Workshop on Extra-Propositional Aspects of Meaning in Computational Linguistics 2012

(ExProM 2012)

Held at the 50th Annual Meeting of the Association for Computational Linguistics 2012 (ACL 2012)

Jeju Island, Korea
13 July 2012

ISBN: 978-1-62276-599-7

Printed from e-media with permission by:

Curran Associates, Inc.
57 Morehouse Lane
Red Hook, NY 12571

proceedings.com

Some format issues inherent in the e-media version may also appear in this print version.

Printed by Curran Associates, Inc. (2012)

Association for Computational Linguistics
209 N. Eighth Street
Stroudsburg, Pennsylvania 18360

Phone: 1-570-476-8006
Fax: 1-570-476-0860

acl@aclweb.org

Additional copies of this publication are available from:

Curran Associates, Inc.
57 Morehouse Lane
Red Hook, NY 12571 USA
Phone: 845-758-0400
Fax: 845-758-2634
Email: curran@proceedings.com
Web: www.proceedings.com

Introduction

Until recently, research in Natural Language Processing (NLP) has focused predominantly on propositional aspects of meaning, such as extracting factual information about who did what to whom. However, understanding language fully also requires awareness and comprehension of Extra-Propositional Aspects of Meaning (EPAM), such as factuality, uncertainty, subjectivity, and irony. The same propositional meaning can be expressed in various linguistic forms reflecting different extra-propositional meaning aspects, e.g.:

- The earthquake adds further threats to the global economy.
- Does the earthquake add further threats to the global economy?
- The earthquake will probably add further threats to the global economy.
- Who could possibly think the earthquake adds further threats to the global economy?
- It has been denied that the earthquake adds further threats to the global economy.

Recently, work on EPAM has received increasing attention in the NLP community, especially in the context of sentiment processing. However, while there is a growing amount of research on phenomena like subjectivity and factuality, other phenomena like the detection of sarcasm have received less attention.

With this workshop we aim to bring together scientists working on EPAM from any area related to computational language learning and processing and thereby help to consolidate this emerging area of research. We received 14 submissions; 10 papers were selected for inclusion in the workshop. The papers cover a wide range of topics, including the detection of factuality, subjectivity and speculation, annotation issues related to EPAM, or cognitive processing and EPAM. Several papers contain empirical studies that take a closer look at the linguistic expression of EPAM and how it relates to what the speaker/writer intends to convey (e.g., the diagnostic correctness in a medical setting) or what the listener/reader understands (e.g., the perceived subjectivity or the influence on opinion forming). An invited talk by Bonnie Webber on "Alternatives and Extra-Propositional Meaning" completes the workshop program.

We would like to thank all authors who submitted papers for the hard work that went into their submissions. We are also extremely grateful to the members of the program committee for their thorough reviews, and to the ACL 2012 organizers, especially the Workshop Chairs Massimo Poesio and Satoshi Sekine. Special thanks to our invited speaker Bonnie Webber and to the PASCAL2 Network for their generous sponsorship of the workshop. This workshop is a follow-up to Negation and Speculation in Natural Language Processing (NeSp-NLP 2010) held in Uppsala, Sweden, in July 2010.

Roser Morante and Caroline Sporleder

Organizers:

Roser Morante, CLiPS - Computational Linguistics, University of Antwerp (Belgium)
Caroline Sporleder, MMCI Cluster of Excellence, Saarland University (Germany)

Program Committee:

Eduardo Blanco, Lymba Corporation (USA)
Johan Bos, University of Groningen (The Netherlands)
Gosse Bouma, University of Groningen (The Netherlands)
Jorge Carrillo de Albornoz, UNED (Spain)
Walter Daelemans, University of Antwerp (Belgium)
Matthew Gerber, University of Virginia (USA)
Roxana Girju, University of Illinois at Urbana-Champaign (USA)
Iris Hendrickx, University of Lisbon (Portugal)
Halil Kilicoglu, Concordia University (Canada)
Maria Liakata, University of Wales (UK)
Katja Markert, University of Leeds (UK)
Erwin Marsi, Norwegian University of Science and Technology (Norway)
David Martínez, NICTA and University of Melbourne (Australia)
Malvina Nissim, University of Bologna (Italy)
Sebastian Padó, University of Heidelberg (Germany)
Sampo Pyysalo, NaCTeM and University of Manchester (UK)
Owen Rambow, Columbia University (USA)
Paolo Rosso, Universidad Politécnica de Valencia (Spain)
Josef Ruppenhofer, Hildesheim University (Germany)
Roser Saurí, Barcelona Media Innovation Center (Spain)
Carlo Strapparava, Fondazione Bruno Kessler (Italy)
György Szarvas, TU Darmstadt (Germany)
Erik Velldal, University of Oslo (Norway)
Anita de Waard, Elsevier Labs (USA)
Bonnie Webber, University of Edinburgh (UK)
Michael Wiegand, Saarland University (Germany)
Sander Wubben, Tilburg University (The Netherlands)

Invited Speaker:

Bonnie Webber, University of Edinburgh

Table of Contents

Conference Program

Friday July 13, 2012

8:45	Welcome
	Morning session
9:00	*Disfluencies as Extra-Propositional Indicators of Cognitive Processing* Kathryn Womack, Wilson McCoy, Cecilia Ovesdotter Alm, Cara Calvelli, Jeff B. Pelz, Pengcheng Shi and Anne Haake
9:30	*How do Negation and Modality Impact on Opinions?* Farah Benamara, Baptiste Chardon, Yannick Mathieu, Vladimir Popescu and Nicholas Asher
10:00	*Linking Uncertainty in Physicians' Narratives to Diagnostic Correctness* Wilson McCoy, Cecilia Ovesdotter Alm, Cara Calvelli, Jeff B. Pelz, Pengcheng Shi and Anne Haake
10:30	Coffee break
11:00	*Factuality Detection on the Cheap: Inferring Factuality for Increased Precision in Detecting Negated Events* Erik Velldal and Jonathon Read
11:30	*Improving Speculative Language Detection using Linguistic Knowledge* Guillermo Moncecchi, Jean-Luc Minel and Dina Wonsever
12:00	*Bridging the Gap Between Scope-based and Event-based Negation/Speculation Annotations: A Bridge Not Too Far* Pontus Stenetorp, Sampo Pyysalo, Tomoko Ohta, Sophia Ananiadou and Jun'ichi Tsujii
12:30	Lunch

Friday July 13, 2012 (continued)

Afternoon session

14:00	PASCAL2 Invited talk by Bonnie Webber: Alternatives and Extra-Propositional Meaning
15:00	*Statistical Modality Tagging from Rule-based Annotations and Crowdsourcing* Vinodkumar Prabhakaran, Michael Bloodgood, Mona Diab, Bonnie Dorr, Lori Levin, Christine D. Piatko, Owen Rambow and Benjamin Van Durme
15:30	Coffee break
16:00	*Annotating the Focus of Negation in terms of Questions Under Discussion* Pranav Anand and Craig Martell
16:30	*Hedge Detection as a Lens on Framing in the GMO Debates: A Position Paper* Eunsol Choi, Chenhao Tan, Lillian Lee, Cristian Danescu-Niculescu-Mizil and Jennifer Spindel
17:00	*Recognizing Arguing Subjectivity and Argument Tags* Alexander Conrad, Janyce Wiebe and Rebecca Hwa
17:30	Discussion

Disfluencies as Extra-Propositional Indicators of Cognitive Processing

Kathryn Womack
Dept. of ASL
& Interpreting Edu.
kaw8159@rit.edu

Wilson McCoy
Dept. of Interactive
Games & Media
wgm4143@rit.edu

Cecilia Ovesdotter Alm
Dept. of English
coagla@rit.edu

Cara Calvelli
College of Health
Sciences & Tech.
cfcscl@rit.edu

Jeff B. Pelz
Center for
Imaging Science
pelz@cis.rit.edu

Pengcheng Shi
Computing &
Information Sciences
spcast@rit.edu

Anne Haake
Computing &
Information Sciences
anne.haake@rit.edu

Rochester Institute of Technology

Abstract

We explore filled pause usage in spontaneous medical narration. Expert physicians viewed images of dermatological conditions and provided a description while working toward a diagnosis. The narratives were analyzed for differences in filled pauses used by attending (experienced) and resident (in-training) physicians and by male and female physicians. Attending physicians described more and used more filled pauses than residents. No difference was found by speaker gender. Acoustic speech features were examined for two types of filled pauses: nasal (e.g. *um*) and non-nasal (e.g. *uh*). Nasal filled pauses were more often followed by longer silent pauses. Scores capturing diagnostic correctness and diagnostic thoroughness for each narrative were compared against filled pauses. The number of filled and silent pauses trends upward as correctness scores increase, indicating a tentative relationship between filled pause usage and expertise. Also, we report on a computational model for predicting types of filled pause.

1 Introduction

Although they are often not consciously realized, disfluencies are common in everyday speech. In an overview of several studies, Fox Tree (1995) estimates that approximately 6% of speech is disfluent. Disfluencies include filled pauses, silent pauses, edited or repeated words, and sounds such as clearing one's throat or click noises. Disfluencies affect the way that listeners comprehend speech in learning situations (Barr, 2003), formulate opinions of the speaker as being more or less fluent (Lövgren and van Doorn, 2005), and even parse grammatically complex sentences (Bailey and Ferreira, 2003).

Since disfluencies are generally absent in written text, they are irrelevant when analyzing text for extra-propositional meaning, such as uncertainty or modality (Vincze et al., 2008, for example). In contrast, when studying meaning in spoken language, disfluencies provide information about a speaker's cognitive state. For example, they might indicate cognitive load, uncertainty, confidence, thoughtfulness, problems in reasoning, or stylistic preferences between individuals or groups of individuals. We study filled pauses (e.g. *um* and *uh*) and leave other disfluency types for future work.

The presence of filled pauses could indicate context-dependent facets of cognitive reasoning processes. We examine filled pauses present in the speech of highly-trained dermatologists who were shown images of dermatological conditions and asked to provide a description and diagnosis. We look at the difference between two different types of filled pauses: those with nasal consonants, such as *um*; and those without nasal consonants, such as *uh*. We build a computational model to confirm findings that nasal and non-nasal filled pauses differ by prosodic and contextual features. In addition, we first compare whether there is a difference between filled pause use for variables such as level of physician expertise and gender. We also examine the relationship of correctness in the diagnostic process with respect to filled pause use.

There is evidence that filled pauses indicate cognitive processing difficulties and could change the speaker's intended meaning or the listener's perceived meaning of an utterance. However, such implicit meanings are severely understudied in previous work, especially in specialized, high-stakes domains such as medical diagnostics. Little is understood about what factors impact the linguistic behavior of using certain filled pauses rather than others, and how the use of filled pauses differs based on level of expertise, gender, or diagnostic correctness. Looking into these differences is useful to form a better understanding of the relationship between language and specialized decision-making processes. More specifically, it is necessary to improve the understanding of how speakers' use of filled pauses differs based on the context of speech and how they change the meaning and reception of speech in extra-propositional ways.

2 Previous Work

Filled pauses in English include monosyllables with and without nasal consonants, such as *um* and *uh* respectively. Filled pauses are most common in unstructured, spontaneous speech, but they are also present in prompted, structured speech; and occur in both monologues and dialogues.

Much research has been done into hedging, negation, and other propositional features that change the meaning or modality of phrases (Morante and Sporleder, in press). Less research has been done into the usage of filled pauses and their relationship to certainty and speculation. It has been shown that disfluencies are used to indicate uncertainty in speakers' forthcoming statements or to indicate that the speaker is engaged in the discourse but working to formulate their response (Brennan and Williams, 1995; Smith and Clark, 1993). These studies found that speakers less confident of their answers take longer to answer and use more disfluencies.

Recent studies have suggested that disfluencies provide meaningful information about the speaker's cognitive or linguistic processes (Arnold et al., 2003; Bortfeld et al., 2001; Corley and Stewart, 2008; Oviatt, 1995, for example), and are unintentional indications that the speaker is having difficulty formulating upcoming speech.

More specifically, it has been shown that the two major categories of filled pauses, i.e. nasal and non-nasal, are specific indicators of the level of cognitive load, with nasal filled pauses indicating higher load and non-nasal filled pauses indicating lower load. Barr (2001) performed an experiment in which a speaker described one of several visible images to a listener who then selected the image being described. In this study as well as in Barr and Seyfiddinipur (2010), listeners focused on a topic that was new to the discourse or exceptionally complex when they heard the speaker say *um*. Although they did not differentiate between nasal and non-nasal filled pauses, Arnold et al. (2003; 2007) found in similar experiments that filled pauses often preceded unfamiliar or complex objects.

There is evidence that speakers use filled pauses to indicate different processing difficulties. Clark and Fox Tree (2002) describe four different filled pauses that are annotated in the corpora they use. These are *uh*, *um*, and their elongated versions *u:h* and *u:m*. They argue that each of these corresponds to a different following pause time with *uh* being followed by the shortest pause time, then *u:h*, *um*, and *u:m* followed by the longest. It is important to note that their primary corpus is the London-Lund Corpus of Spoken English, in which the pause times were annotated based on the transcriber's estimate of pause time in units of "one light foot" or "one stress unit" (Clark and Fox Tree, 2002, p. 80) rather than measured in seconds.[1]

However, studies on filled pauses by Barr (2001) and Smith and Clark (1993) measured the duration of silent pauses in seconds and confirm that *um* was followed by longer silent pauses than *uh*. The hypothesis suggested by Barr, Clark and Fox Tree, and Smith and Clark is that *uh* indicates a minor delay and lower level of cognitive difficulty while *um* indicates a major delay due to higher level of difficulty in speech planning and production.

On the other hand, a study by O'Connell and Kowal (2005) refuted the findings of Clark and Fox Tree and showed that specific filled pauses could not predict pause time in their corpus of TV interviews. O'Connell and Kowal's corpus was six interviews conducted by various TV personnel with

[1]The difference between listeners' perception of duration and actual duration is an important one because perceptual and actual duration do not always match (Megyesi and Gustafson-Capkova, 2002; Spinos et al., 2002).

Hillary Clinton because these "professional speakers" (O'Connell and Kowal, 2005, p. 560) should be more likely to use filled pauses according to convention. However, speech in public TV interviews is likely to be pre-planned and highly self-monitored by the speakers, and it may not be appropriate to consider this situation a model for spontaneous, less formal, and less public speech. It has been shown that rate and use of filled pauses can vary widely within certain fields (Schachter et al., 1991), in situations that are more or less structured (Oviatt, 1995), and depending on the formality of the situational context (Bortfeld et al., 2001).

3 Data, Annotation, and Methods

Data were acquired from a study involving 16 dermatologists, including 12 attending physicians and 4 residents. The participants were evenly split for gender. These physicians were shown 50 images of different dermatological conditions and asked to provide a description and diagnosis of each. In a modification of the Master-Apprentice scenario (Beyer and Holtzblatt, 1997), each observer explained his or her thoughts and processes to a student who was silent. These are monologues; however, the Master has the feeling of interaction and of dialogue.

Audio of each description was recorded while eye-movements were tracked. The relationship between eye-movements and extra-propositional features will be the topic of a later study. The audio files were manually single-annotated and time-aligned at the word level in Praat, a software for acoustic and phonetic analysis (Boersma, 2001). A section of the spoken narrative with time-alignment is pictured in Figure 1. Praat and Python scripts were used to computationally extract measurements of pitch, intensity, and duration for words, silent pauses, and narratives. In total, there were 800 audio-recorded narratives. At this time, 707 of these narratives have been time-aligned and annotated and only these are used in this study.

Four transcribers worked independently on time-alignment, and they were given instructions by one coordinator. Every spoken token was included in the transcriptions, including filled pauses, extra-linguistic sounds such as clicks, repairs, and silent pauses. Annotators were instructed to mark only

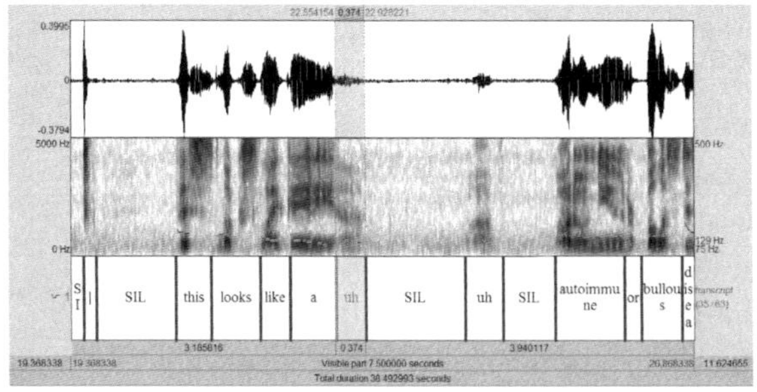

Figure 1: Screenshot of the program Praat which was used to time-align each narrative and extract acoustic prosodic information about the physicians' speech.

silent pauses that were longer than 30 milliseconds, because it has been shown that pauses under 20-30 ms are not consistently perceived by listeners in discourse (Kirsner et al., 2002; Lövgren and van Doorn, 2005).

After word-level time-alignment, each narrative was independently annotated by three expert dermatologists who did not participate in the original data elicitation procedure. Each narrative was examined for *medical lesion morphology* (the description of the condition), *differential diagnosis* (possible diagnostic conditions), and *final diagnosis* (the diagnosis that the observer found most likely). These independent experts annotated the physicians' diagnostic correctness for the three steps of the diagnostic process. They annotated medical lesion morphology as *correct*, *incorrect*, *correct but incomplete*, or *none*, indicating that no medical morphology was given. Final diagnosis was labeled as *correct*, *incorrect*, or *none*, and differential diagnosis was rated as *yes*, *no*, or *no differential given*. An analysis of the annotated data set is discussed by McCoy et al. (Forthcoming 2012).

4 Results and Discussion

4.1 Types of Filled Pauses

Nasal filled pauses included *hm* and *um* and non-nasal filled pauses included *ah*, *er*, and *uh*. We analyzed nasal and non-nasal filled pauses as groups rather than each individual filled pause because the number of filled pauses within each category was not balanced. Higher token counts of *uh* and *um* were identified, with fewer *ah*, *er*, and *hm* filled pauses. In comparing use of nasal and non-nasal filled pauses,

FPs	No.	Dur.	St. Dev.	%
hm	78	0.48 s	0.20	2%
um	1439	0.51 s	0.19	36%
Total (nasal)	1517	0.50 s	0.19	38%
ah	23	0.46 s	0.23	1%
er	9	0.26 s	0.09	<1%
uh	2401	0.36 s	0.16	61%
Total (non-nasal)	2433	0.36 s	0.16	62%
Total (all)	3950	0.42 s	0.19	100%

Table 1: Total number of each type of filled pause (FPs) with mean duration in seconds, standard deviation of the mean duration, and percentage of all filled pauses.

we considered all 707 narratives. The number of tokens and average duration for each filled pause is given in Table 1.

The average filled pause duration was slightly longer for nasal than for non-nasal, likely due to the segmental quality.

In total, 38% of the filled pauses in our data set are nasal. However, observers vary widely in their individual usage, from one observer who used 22 non-nasal (10%) and 189 nasal (90%) filled pauses to an observer at the other extreme who used 562 non-nasal (97%) and only 19 nasal (3%) filled pauses. Some people seem to have a tendency to use one type of filled pause over the other.

Clark and Fox Tree (2002) found that nasal filled pauses were more often followed by silent pauses and that those silences were on average longer than that of non-nasal filled pauses. Our data are consistent with this as shown in Tables 2 and 3,[2] and Figure 2. Of the total nasal filled pauses, 70% were followed by a silent pause, whereas only 41% of non-nasal filled pauses were followed by a silent pause.

The mean duration of silent pauses following nasal filled pauses was 1.5 s while non-nasal was 1.1 s, which indicates a difference significant enough that it could be recognized by a listener. These findings show that nasal filled pauses are good indicators of continuing delay, which supports Clark and Fox Tree's hypothesis that nasal and non-nasal filled pauses are used to indicate different levels of difficulty in speech planning. Taken with the results of experiments by Barr (2001) that nasal filled pauses are more often used before a topic that is relatively

[2]The data were analyzed using two-sample t-tests assuming unequal variances.

	Nasal (*hm, um*)	Non-nasal (*ah, er, uh*)	*p*
Dur. of FPs	0.50 s	0.36 s	< 0.01
Dur. of FPs + SILs	2.46 s	1.37 s	< 0.01
No. of FPs	1517	2433	n/a

Table 2: Mean duration in seconds of filled pauses (FPs), and mean duration of the filled pause including the span of any preceding and following silences. If there were no silences, only the duration of the filled pause was used to calculate the mean.

	Nasal (*hm, um*)	Non-nasal (*ah, er, uh*)	*p*
Dur. of pre. SILs	1.19 s	1.15 s	0.4
No. of pre. SILs	1167	1197	n/a
Dur. of foll. SILs	1.50 s	1.07 s	< 0.01
No. of foll. SILs	1059	1006	n/a

Table 3: Mean duration in seconds of silent pauses (SILs) preceding filled pauses, silent pauses following filled pauses, and the number of tokens for each. Durations were only considered if there was a silence, so the number of silences was different for each calculation.

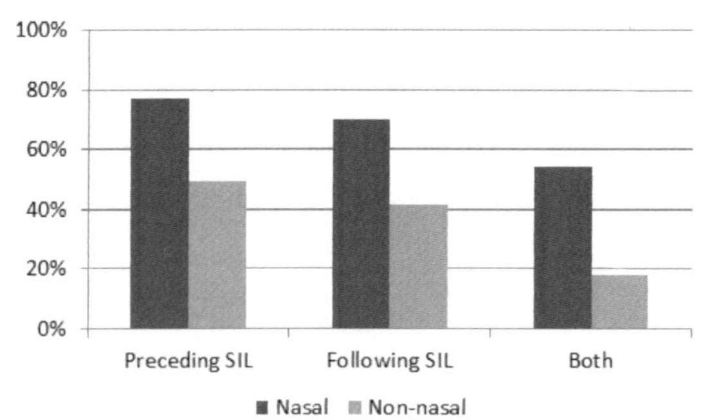

Figure 2: The percentage of nasal and non-nasal filled pauses with a preceding silent pause, following silent pause, and a silent pause both preceding and following.

complex or new to discourse, it seems that nasal filled pauses indicate a higher level of cognitive difficulty than non-nasal filled pauses.

In their previously-mentioned study, Clark and Fox Tree also found that nasal filled pauses were more often preceded by delays and that those delays were longer. Similarly, in our data 77% of the nasal filled pauses were preceded by silences, compared with 49% of non-nasal.

No difference was found in the mean duration of preceding silences, however. Although this conclusion is tentative, it seems that the duration of the preceding pause could be the maximum length of silence a speaker feels is permissible before needing to indicate their continuing participation in the discourse. This supports Jefferson's (1989) findings of a "standard maximum silence" of around 1 second in discourse. At that point, the speaker could need to signal that they have more to say, using a nasal filled pause if they anticipate a long delay or a non-nasal filled pause if they anticipate a shorter delay. The longer duration of surrounding silent pauses for nasal filled pauses also supports the conclusion that they indicate higher cognitive load and more preplanning. This critical finding highlights the importance of considering filled pauses in computational modeling and hint at their potential usefulness across phenomena of extra-propositional meaning.

4.2 Gender

Traditional stereotypes have held that women are less confident speakers than men. When women and men use the same number of hedge words or modifiers, women are judged more harshly as sounding passive or uncertain (Bradley, 1981). Although different rates and ratios of filled pauses were identified, Acton (2011), Binnenpoorte et al. (2005), and Bortfeld et al. (2001) all found that women used a lower rate of filled pauses than men. Acton also found that women consistently used a higher ratio of nasal filled pauses.

Our data were analyzed at the level of diagnostic narrative based on the means of: number of filled pauses, filled pauses per second, the percentage of filled pauses (i.e. the rate per 100 words), the number of nasal filled pauses, and the percentage of nasal filled pauses. The difference between the means was not statistically significant, confirmed by the computed *p*-score.[3] Hence, our data do not support a difference in men's and women's use of filled pauses.

There are several possible explanations for this. For example, it has been shown that women tend to be more conscious of their speaking style than men because they are aware of the stereotyping mentioned previously (Gordon, 1994), and they may make more effort to speak clearly. Acton (2011) and Bortfeld et al. (2001) noted different usage of filled pauses by men and women in different situations. Whereas our results point to gender neutrality and refute the common gender bias as well as findings of previous studies, we recognize that our results could reflect that this study involved a largely homogeneous professional and educational group. The studies mentioned thus far used corpora consisting of casual conversations in various situations with individuals of various backgrounds. Further research into gender differences in expert fields could clarify this factor further.

4.3 Level of Expertise

Our data were analyzed based on the means per narrative, similar to Section 4.2, but comparing levels of expertise (attending versus resident physicians). Attending physicians' narratives had a longer mean duration and significantly more words. Attending physicians also used more filled pauses, a higher rate of filled pauses per 100 words, and a higher percentage of nasal filled pauses (see Table 4).[4]

One probable explanation for the difference is that the experienced attendings noticed more about the image, leading them to give more information about their thought processes and go into more detail than residents. It is possible also that the attendings' experience could have provided them with a larger conceptual space and options to explore. This explains the longer narrative time and the higher number of words used. Many of the dermatological terms used are highly complex and may require explanation on the part of the observer, and other stud-

[3]The mean of each category was determined for each observer, and then analyzed using a two-sample t-test. In total, we had 355 narratives from males and 352 from females.

[4]These results were calculated using the mean of each observer and each narrative. A paired t-test was used to compare means for residents on each image against means for attendings on each image.

For Narratives	Attendings' Means	Residents' Means	p
Total Dur.	46.1 s	33.8 s	< 0.01
No. of Words	85.7	50.9	< 0.01
No. of FPs	6.3	1.9	< 0.01
% FPs	8%	4%	< 0.01
% Nasal FPs	0.4%	0.2%	< 0.01

Table 4: Analysis considered, at the narrative level, attending and resident physicians' mean total duration, number of words (including filled and silent pauses), number of filled pauses (FPs), percentage of filled pauses of total words (total words includes pauses; without pauses, this rate would be higher), and percentage of nasal filled pauses of total filled pauses.

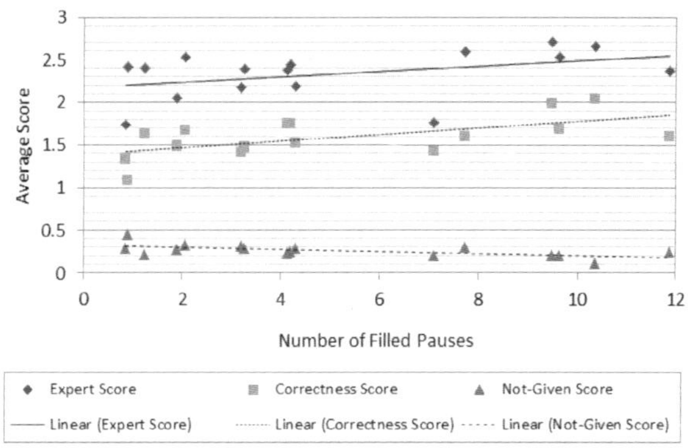

Figure 3: Average number of filled pauses per narrative by observer (y-axis) against the holistic expert score, correctness score, and not-given score (x-axis).

ies have found that the filled pause rate increases as the utterance length increases (Oviatt, 1995; Bortfeld et al., 2001), so one would expect to see more filled pauses used in longer descriptions.

One issue with our data is that the number of attending physicians and the number of resident physicians is not balanced. We had 592 narratives done by 12 attendings and 115 done by 4 residents. All values were calculated using means so the values are not weighted based on the number of narratives analyzed. However, we have previously mentioned that personal preference plays a role in the usage of filled pauses, and we have a wider variety of attending observers than resident observers. It could be that our resident observers happened to be the kinds of people who do not use many filled pauses.

4.4 Diagnostic Correctness

Three scores were determined for each narrative. The first score was the *holistic expert score* provided by the expert annotators, based on "relevancy, thoroughness, and accuracy" of each narrative from 1 to 3 with 3 being the best. The second score was an overall *correctness score* which spanned from 0 to 3, with one-third of a point given per independent annotator for each step (i.e. medical lesion morphology, differential diagnosis, and final diagnosis) if *correct* and $\frac{1}{3} * 0.5$ points given for *correct but incomplete*. The last score was the *not-given score* which, similar to the correctness score, spanned from 0 to 3 with one-third of a point given per annotator for each step if the original observer did not provide that information.[5]

Correlation between these three scores and the number or rate of words, filled pauses, and silent pauses was not strong enough to make predictions, indicating that more factors than just the scores should be considered. However, certain trends were evident. As the holistic expert and correctness scores improved, the means of narratives' total duration in seconds and total number of words also increased. This finding, combined with the fact that experienced physicians spoke more and had higher average correctness and expert scores, indicates that verbal behavior can reflect both heightened conceptual knowledge and level of expertise.

The number of filled pauses per narrative, number of silent pauses per narrative, and the total duration of filled and silent pauses (per narrative) also increased as the holistic expert and correctness scores improved and the not-given score decreased. The graph of filled pauses in Figure 3 indicates that the increase in the number of filled and silent pauses involve more cognitive processing. That the not-given score tends to inversely decrease could indicate very little cognitive processing (e.g., if an observer was so unsure that they did not even hazard a guess).

The number and percentage of nasal filled pauses, as opposed to non-nasal filled pauses, increased at

[5]There was not a strong correlation between the holistic expert, correctness, and not-given scores, but each score measured different criteria. The mean holistic expert score was 2.3 with a standard deviation of 0.5; the mean correctness score was 1.6 with a standard deviation of 0.8; and the mean not-given score was 0.26 with a standard deviation of 0.16.

a slightly higher rate as the holistic expert and correctness scores increased. This could indicate that nasal filled pauses indicate a higher cognitive load and therefore more consideration in the decision-making process. However, as discussed in Section 4.1, this corpus has more non-nasal than nasal filled pauses and some observers have a particular preference, so this would need to be controlled and investigated further.

5 Computational Model of Filled Pauses Based on Speech Features

A computational model was developed to classify filled pauses as either nasal or non-nasal,[6] based on features discussed in our analysis and in previous work. This model performs above a majority class baseline, supporting our findings that there are differences between the two types of filled pauses, given the features that we have examined, which can be captured by a computational model.

The features considered for classification were total duration and number of words in the narrative; duration, intensity, mean pitch, minimum pitch, and maximum pitch of the filled pause;[7] the filled pause's time and word position in the narrative; time and word position as a percentage of the total narrative; and length of silent pauses[8] on each side of the filled pause. The CFS subset evaluation features selection algorithm was first applied. The filled pause duration, maximum pitch, left silence length, and right silence length were maintained as features for classification; other features were not used further.

The widely used J48 decision tree algorithm in Weka[9] was used to classify our data, which allowed us to visualize our model. The experimental approach was guided by the relatively small size of the dataset. We wanted to avoid over- or under-interpretation of results based on just a small held-out test set. The data were shuffled and partitioned differently during tuning and testing to ensure distinct identities of the data splits so that parameters were not tuned on test folds. The algorithm's parameters were tuned using 5-fold cross-validation; the best-performing fold's parameters were chosen. The data were then shuffled anew and split into 10 folds with each fold being the test set for one experimental run. Results are reported on the final 10-fold cross-validation case.

		Predicted	
		Nasal	Non-nasal
Actual	Nasal	900	617
	Non-nasal	462	1971

Table 5: Confusion matrix of classification results.

The baseline for this model was 62% because the majority class, non-nasal filled pauses, comprised that percentage of the data set. Our model correctly classified 73% of the instances, performing 11% above the baseline. A confusion matrix of the classifier output is shown in Table 5. The model performs best for non-nasal filled pauses, likely because they are more common.

The output of the decision tree indicated that duration of the filled pause was the most important feature. As discussed in Section 4.1, this corresponds with our previous statistical findings as well as those of Clark and Fox Tree (2002) that there is a difference in duration of filled pauses. The next most important features were the left and right silence lengths, also supported by our analysis as well as by Clark and Fox Tree (2002) and Barr (2001). The last selected feature was the maximum pitch of the filled pause, possibly due to phonemic qualities.

This computational model mirrors the findings of Section 4.1 that the duration of filled pauses and of surrounding silent pauses are a differentiating factor between nasal and non-nasal filled pauses and that the contextual surroundings of each filled pause type are different. The finding that the two distinct types of filled pauses behave differently in this domain could also aid language processing systems for clinicians in the medical field. Further research into filled pause and other speech phenomena in each step of the diagnostic process (i.e. medical lesion morphology, differential diagnosis, and final diagnosis) could also be explored in future work.

[6] We also made a fine-grained model to classify specific filled pauses *ah*, *er*, *hm*, *uh*, and *um*. It had 70% accuracy but was generally unable to identify the least-often occurring *ah*, *er*, and *hm* filled pauses, so it is not reported on here.

[7] Pitch features were extracted considering gender: 75-300 Hz for men and a 100-500 Hz for women.

[8] If there was no silence, the value was 0.

[9] See http://www.cs.waikato.ac.nz/ml/weka/.

6 Conclusion

The results of this study underscore the need for further research into the production of disfluencies, especially in decision making situations and in specialized fields such as dermatology. Future work will further explore their connection with highly relevant extra-propositional meaning phenomena in diagnostic verbal behaviors such as certainty, confidence, correctness, and thoroughness.

This study has shown that the two main types of filled pauses, nasal and non-nasal, differ in their usage. Nasal filled pauses are more likely to be preceded and followed by silent pauses, and these following silent pauses are more likely to be longer. These findings are reinforced by the computational model which identified the duration of the filled pause, duration of surrounding silences, and pitch as important for classification of filled pause type.

That longer and more frequent silent pauses surround nasal filled pauses supports the hypothesis that nasal filled pauses indicate a higher level of cognitive load (Clark and Fox Tree, 2002) or a topic that is new to the discourse or unusually complex (Barr, 2001; Barr and Seyfiddinipur, 2010).

The lack of differences in use of filled pauses by speaker gender given the differences found by Acton (2011), Binnenpoorte et al. (2005), and Bortfeld et al. (2001) shows that more research is needed to understand gender variation in speech.

Another finding was that level of expertise influenced the use of filled pauses and overall narrative length. On average, attending physicians spoke longer, said more, used more filled pauses, and had a higher percentage of nasal filled pauses. Attending physicians also had slightly higher holistic expert and correctness scores and were more likely to provide medical lesion morphology, differential diagnosis, and final diagnosis. We believe that attending physicians likely noticed more about the images due to their experience.

The differences by level of expertise (in our study, between attending and resident physicians) need to be verified and compared with more data and in non-medical fields. The differences could also be related to teaching experience of the attending physicians, so further research could compare experienced physicians who are also teachers with those who are not, and if their speaking style affects students' comprehension. In general, differences in linguistic behaviors in relation to levels of expertise deserve more research, and might have long-term implications for development of clinical decision-support and training systems.

The information used by the physicians in our study was limited; they were only shown images of dermatological conditions without being able to examine the patient, run diagnostic tests, or have a patient history. This may have changed their the behavior, along with factors such as the difficulty of diagnosis of each image and their role in the Master-Apprentice scenario. Understanding how these variables affect the diagnostic process of physicians could help us understand how disfluencies are impacted by the contexts of diagnostic decision-making.

The differences found between the use of filled pauses based on level of expertise and on the correctness of narratives seem to indicate that filled pauses could provide partial information about the experts' decision-making process as well as level of confidence and certainty. This is especially important in the medical domain in order to understand how physicians' verbal behaviors are interpreted by other physicians as well as by patients and students.

We recently collected a similar, larger data set and we plan to further examine differences based on expertise in this new corpus. In the recent data collection, observers were also asked to rate their level of certainty about the diagnosis. This provides the opportunity to examine the relationship between disfluencies and certainty. We have eye-tracking data for both studies and future work will also look at eye-movements in relation to the use of filled and silent pauses, certainty, expertise level, and cognitive load.

Acknowledgements

Supported in part by NIH 1 R21 LM010039-01A1, NSF IIS-0941452, RIT GCCIS Seed Funding, and RIT Research Computing (http://rc.rit.edu). We thank Lowell A. Goldsmith, M.D. and the anonymous reviewers for their comments, and Dr. Rubén Proaño for input on statistical analysis.

References

Eric K. Acton. 2011. On gender differences in the distribution of um and uh. *University of Pennsylvania Working Papers in Linguistics*, 17(2).

Jennifer E. Arnold, Maria Fagnano, and Michael K. Tanenhaus. 2003. Disfluencies signal theee, um, new information. *Journal of Psycholinguistic Research*, 32(1):25–36.

Jennifer E. Arnold, Carla L. Hudson Kam, and Michael K. Tanenhaus. 2007. If you say thee uh you are describing something hard: The on-line attribution of disfluency during reference comprehension. *Journal of Experimental Psychology: Learning, Memory, and Cognition*, 33(5):914–930.

Karl G.D. Bailey and Fernanda Ferreira. 2003. Disfluencies affect the parsing of garden-path sentences. *Journal of Memory and Language*, 49:183–200.

Dale J. Barr and Mandana Seyfiddinipur. 2010. The role of fillers in listener attributes for speaker disfluency. *Language and Cognitive Processes*, 25(4):441–455.

Dale J. Barr. 2001. Trouble in mind: Paralinguistic indices of effort and uncertainty in communication. *Oralité and gestualité: Communication Multimodale, Interaction*, pages 597–600.

Dale J. Barr. 2003. Paralinguistic correlates of conceptual structure. *Psychonomic Bulletin & Review*, 10(2):462–467.

Hugh Beyer and Karen Holtzblatt. 1997. *Contextual Design: Defining Customer-Centered Systems*. Morgan Kaufmann.

Diana Binnenpoorte, Christophe Van Bael, Els den Os, and Lou Boves. 2005. Gender in everyday speech and language: A corpus-based study. *Interspeech*, pages 2213–2216.

Paul Boersma. 2001. Praat, a system for doing phonetics by computer. *Glot International*, pages 341–345.

Heather Bortfeld, Silvia D. Leon, Johnathan E. Bloom, Michael F. Schober, and Susan E. Brennan. 2001. Disfluency rates in conversation: Effects of age, relationship, topic, role, and gender. *Language and Speech*, 44(2):123–147.

Patricia Hayes Bradley. 1981. The folk-linguistics of women's speech: an empirical investigation. *Communication Monographs*, 48(1):78–91.

Susan E. Brennan and Maurice Williams. 1995. The feeling of another's knowing: Prosody and filled pauses as cues to listeners about the metacognitive states of speakers. *Journal of Memory and Language*, 34:383–398.

Herbert H. Clark and Jean E. Fox Tree. 2002. Using uh and um in spontaneous speaking. *Cognition*, 84:73–111.

Martin Corley and Oliver W. Stewart. 2008. Hesitation disfluencies in spontaneous speech: The meaning of um. *Lang. and Linguistics Compass*, 2(4):589–602.

Jean E. Fox Tree. 1995. The effects of false starts and repetitions on the processing of subsequent words in spontaneous speech. *Journal of Memory and Language*, 34:709–738.

Elizabeth Gordon. 1994. Sex differences in language: Another explanation? *American Speech*, 69(2):215–221.

Gail Jefferson. 1989. Notes on a possible metric which provides for a 'standard maximum' silence of approximately one second in conversation. In Derek Roger and Peter Bull, editors, *Conversation*, chapter 8, pages 166–196. Multilingual Matters, Clevedon, UK.

Kim Kirsner, John Dunn, Kathryn Hird, Tim Parkin, and Craig Clark. 2002. Time for a pause. *Proc. of the 9th Australian Int'l. Conf. on Speech Science & Tech.*, pages 52–57.

Tobias Lövgren and Jan van Doorn. 2005. Influence of manipulation of short silent pause duration on speech fluency. *Proceedings of DiSS05*, pages 123–126.

Wilson McCoy, Cecilia Ovesdotter Alm, Cara Calvelli, Jeff Pelz, Pengcheng Shi, and Anne Haake. Forthcoming-2012. Linking uncertainty in physicians' narratives to diagnostic correctness. *Proc. of the ExProM 2012 Workshop.*

Beata Megyesi and Sofia Gustafson-Capkova. 2002. Production and perception of pauses and their linguistic context in read and spontaneous speech in Swedish. *ICSLP 7.*

Roser Morante and Caroline Sporleder. in press. Modality and negation: An introduction to the special issue. *Computational Linguistics*.

Daniel C. O'Connell and Sabine Kowal. 2005. uh and um revisited: Are they interjections for signaling delay? *Journal of Psycholinguistic Research*, 34(6):555–576.

Sharon Oviatt. 1995. Predicting and managing spoken disfluencies during human-computer interaction. *Computer Speech and Language*, 9:19–35.

Stanley Schachter, Nicholas Christenfeld, Bernard Ravina, and Frances Bilous. 1991. Speech disfluency and the structure of knowledge. *JPSP*, 60(3):362–367.

Vicki L. Smith and Herbert H. Clark. 1993. On the course of answering questions. *Journal of Memory and Language*, 32:25–38.

Anna-Marie R. Spinos, Daniel C. O'Connell, and Sabine Kowal. 2002. An empirical investigation of pause notation. *Pragmatics*, 12(1):1–9.

Veronika Vincze, György Szarvas, Richárd Farkas, György Móra, and János Csirik. 2008. The bioscope corpus: Biomedical texts annotated for uncertainty, negation, and their scopes. *BMC Bioinformatics*, 9.

How do Negation and Modality Impact on Opinions?

Farah Benamara[1] **Baptiste Chardon**[1,2] **Yannick Mathieu**[3] **Vladimir Popescu**[1] **Nicholas Asher**[1]
[1] IRIT, Univ. Toulouse, France
{benamara,popescu,asher}@irit.fr

[2] Synapse Développement, Toulouse, France
baptiste.chardon@synapse-fr.com

[3] LLF-CNRS, Paris, France
yannick.mathieu@linguist.jussieu.fr

Abstract

In this paper, we propose to study the effects of negation and modality on opinion expressions. Based on linguistic experiments informed by native speakers, we distill these effects according to the type of modality and negation. We show that each type has a specific effect on the opinion expression in its scope: both on the polarity and the strength for negation, and on the strength and/or the degree of certainty for modality. The empirical results reported in this paper provide a basis for future opinion analysis systems that have to compute the sentiment orientation at the sentence or at the clause level. The methodology we used for deriving this basis was applied for French but it can be easily instantiated for other languages like English.

1 Introduction

Negation and modality are complex linguistic phenomena widely studied in philosophy, logic and linguistics. From an NLP perspective, their analysis has recently become a new research area. In fact, they can be beneficial to several NLP applications needing deep language understanding, such as sentiment analysis, textual entailment, dialogue systems and question answering. Handling negation and modality in NLP applications roughly involves two sub-tasks: (i) identifying these expressions and their scope and (ii) analyzing their effect on meaning and how this effect can help to improve text understanding. In this paper, we deal with the second task focusing on fine-grained sentiment analysis of French opinion texts.

Negation and modality function as operators modifying the meaning of the phrases in their scope. Negation can be used to deny or reject statements. It is grammatically expressed via a variety of forms: using *prefixes* ("un-", "il-"), *suffixes* ("-less"), *negator words*, such as "not" and *negative polarity items* (NPIs), which are words or idioms that appear in negative sentences, but not in their affirmative counterparts, or in questions, but not in assertions, for example "any", "anything", "ever". Negation can also be expressed using some nouns or verbs where negation is part of their lexical semantics (as "abate" and "eliminate"), or expressed implicitly without using any negative words, as in "this restaurant was below my expectations". Modality can be used to express possibility, necessity, permission, obligation or desire. It is grammatically expressed via adverbial phrases ("maybe", "certainly"), conditional verbal moods and some verbs ("must", "can", "may"). Adjectives and nouns can also express modality (e.g. "a probable cause").

Negation and modality can aggregate in a variety of ways: (1) multiple negatives, e.g, "This restaurant never fails to disappoint on flavor". In some languages, double negatives cancel the effect of negation, while in negative-concord languages like French, double negations usually intensify the effect of negation. (2) cumulative modalities, as in "You definitely must see this movie" and (3) both negation and modality, as in "you should not go see this movie".

Several reports have shown that negations and modalities are sentiment-relevant (Wiegand et al., 2010). Kennedy and Inkpen (2006) point out that negations are more sentiment-relevant than diminishers. Wilson et al. (2009) show that modalities as well as negations are good cues for opinion identification. Given that the sentiment-relevance of negations and modalities is an established fact, this paper aims to go further by exploring how this relevance is distilled according to the semantics of each operator.

To this end, we first study several taxonomies along with their associated categories of both modality and negation given by the linguistic literature. Among these categories, we decide to choose the categories of (Godard, to appear) for negations. For modalities, we rely on the categories of (Larreya, 2004) and (Portner, 2009). We thus distinguish three types of negation: *negative operators*, *negative quantifiers* and *lexical negations* and three types of modality: *buletic*, *epistemic* and *deontic*. We show that each type has a specific effect on the opinion expression in its scope: both on the polarity and the strength for negation, and on the strength and/or the degree of certainty for modality. These effects are structured as a set of hypotheses that we empirically validated via several linguistic experiments informed by native speakers. This evaluation methodology has already been used in sentiment analysis. Greene and Resnik (2009) chose psycholinguistic methods for assessing the connection between sentence structure and implicit sentiment. Taboada et al. (2011) used Mechanical Turk to check subjective dictionaries for consistency.

The empirical results reported in this paper provide a basis for future opinion analysis systems that have to compute the sentiment orientation at the sentence or at the clause level. The methodology we used for deriving this basis was applied for French but it can be easily instantiated for other languages like English. In this paper, all examples are in French along with their direct translation in English. Note however that there are substantial semantic differences between the two languages.

2 Related Work

2.1 Negation in Sentiment Analysis

Research efforts using negation in sentiment analysis can be grouped according to three main criteria: the effect of negation on opinion expressions, the types of negation used and the method employed to update the prior polarity of opinion expressions.

According to the first criterion, most approaches treat negation as polarity reversal (Polanyi and Zaenen, 2006; Wilson et al., 2005; Moilanen and Pulman, 2007; Choi and Cardie, 2008). However, negation cannot be reduced to reversing polarity. For example, if we assume that the score of the adjective "excellent" is +3, then the opinion score in "this student is not excellent" cannot be -3. It rather means that the student is not good enough. Hence, dealing with negation requires to go beyond polarity reversal. Liu and Seneff (2009) propose a linear additive model that treats negations as modifying adverbs. In the same way, in (Taboada et al., 2011), the negation of an opinion expression shifts the value of its score to the opposite polarity by a fixed amount. Thus a +2 adjective is negated to a -2, but the negation of a very negative adjective is only slightly positive. Based on (Taboada et al., 2011)'s shift model, Yessenalina and Cardie (2011) propose to represent each word as a matrix and combine words using iterated matrix multiplication, which allows for modeling both additive (for negations) and multiplicative (for intensifiers) semantic effects. In our framework, we assume, as in (Liu and Seneff, 2009) and (Taboada et al., 2011), that negation affects both the polarity and the strength of an opinion expression. However, unlike other studies, we distill that effect depending on the type of the negation.

Two main types of negation were studied in the literature: negators such as "not" and content word negators such as "eliminate" (Choi and Cardie, 2008). Wilson et al. (2009) also consider negators and in addition distinguish between positive polarity shifters and negative polarity shifters since they only reverse a particular polarity type. Few studies take into account other types of negation. Among them, Taboada et al. (2011) treat NPIs (as well as modalities) as "irrealis blockers" by ignoring the semantic orientation of the word in their scope. For example, the opinion word "good" will just be ignored in "any good movie in this theater". We think that ignoring NPIs is not suitable and a more accurate analysis is needed. In addition, to our knowledge, no studies have investigated the effect of multiple negatives on opinions.

Finally, methods dealing with negation can be classified into three categories (Wiegand et al.,

2010). In *the shallow approach,* negation is embedded into a bag-of-words model which is then used by supervised machine-learning algorithms for polarity classification (Pang et al.2002; Ng et al. 2006). This method, rather simple, seems linguistically inaccurate and increases the feature space with more sparse features. The second approach concerns a *local contextual analysis of valence shifter terms* where negation modifies the prior scores of those terms (Taboada et al., 2011; Wilson et al., 2009). The last approach uses *semantic composition* where the polarities of words within the sentence are aggregated (Moilanen and Pulman, 2007). In this paper, we provide a way of treating negation and modality in a semantic composition framework.

2.2 Modality in Sentiment Analysis

In sentiment analysis, the presence of modalities can be used as a feature in a machine learning setting for sentence-level opinion classification. Among the few research efforts in this direction, Wilson et al. (2009) use a list of modal words. In (Kobayakawa et al., 2009), modalities are defined in a flat taxonomy: request, recommendation, desire, will, judgment, etc. According to the reported results, the gain brought by the modalities seems difficult to assess. However, to our knowledge, no work has investigated how modality impacts on opinions.

In NLP, modality is less addressed than other linguistic operators, such as negations. Most of the computational studies involving modality are focused on: (i) building annotated resources in terms of factuality information and (ii) uncertainty modeling and hedge detection in texts. Among annotated resources, we cite the FactBank corpus (Saurí and Pustejovsky, 2009) and the BioScope corpus (Vincze et al., 2008). In the second research strand, the efforts go from detecting uncertainty in texts (Rubin, 2010), to finding hedges and their scopes in specialized corpora (Vincze et al., 2008; Ganter and Strube, 2009; Zhao et al., 2010). However, there is only partial overlapping between hedges and modal constructions. Hedges are linguistic means whereby the authors show that they cannot back their opinions with facts. Thus, hedges include certain modal constructions (especially epistemic), along with other markers such as indirect speech, e.g., "According to certain researchers,...". On the other hand, there are modal constructions which are not hedges, e.g. when expressing a factual possibility, without uncertainty on behalf of the speaker, e.g. *may* in "These insects may play a part in the reproduction of plants as well".

3 Dealing with Negation

Negation has been well studied in linguistics (Horn, 1989; Swart, 2010; Giannakidou, 2011). For French, we cite (Muller, 1991; Moeschler, 1992; Corblin and Tovena, 2003) and (Godard, to appear)'s work as part of the "Grande Grammaire du français" project (Abeillé and Godard, 2010). Our treatment of negation is based on the lexical-syntactic classification of (Godard, to appear) that distinguishes three types of negation in French:

- *Negative operators*, denoted by `NEG`: they are the adverbs "pas" ("not"), "plus" ("no more"), "non" ("no one"), the preposition "sans" ("without") and the conjunction "ni" ("neither"). These operators always appear alone in the sentence and they cannot be combined with each other.

- *Negative quantifiers*, denoted by `NEG_quant`, express both a negation and a quantification. They are, for example, the nouns and pronouns "aucun" ("none"), "nul" ("no"), "personne" ("nobody"), "rien" ("nothing") and the adverbs "jamais" ("never") and "aucunement"/"nullement" ("in no way"). `Neg_quant` have three main properties: (i) they can occur in positive sentences (that is not negated), particularly in interrogatives, when they are employed as indefinite or when they appear after the relative pronoun "que" ("that") (ii) in negative contexts, they are always associated to the adverb "ne" ("not") and (iii) they can be combined with each other as well as with negative operators. Here are some examples of this type of negation extracted form our corpus: "on ne s'ennuie jamais" ("you will never be bored"), "je ne recommande cette série à personne" ("I do not recommend this movie to anyone").

- *Lexical negations* denoted by `NEG_lex` which are implicit negative words, such as "manque de" ("lack of"), "absence de"("absence of"), "carence" ("deficiency"), "manquer de" ("to lack"), " dénué de" ("deprived of"). NEG_lex can be combined with each other as well as with the two previous types of negation.

This classification does not cover words such as *few* or *only*, since we consider them as weak intensifiers (strength diminishers) rather than negations.

For each opinion expression exp, OP(exp) indicates that the expression exp is in the scope of the negation OP $\in$ NEG, NEG_quant, NEG_lex. Multiple negations are denoted by OP_i(OP_j((exp))). In French, there are at most three negative words in a multiple negative. However, this case is relatively rare in opinion texts; this is why, we only deal with two negatives. Usually, multiple negatives preserve polarity, except for those composed of NEG_lex and NEG_quant or NEG which cancel the effect of NEG_lex. For example, in "manque de goût" ("lack of taste"), i.e NEG_lex(taste), the polarity is negative, while in "il ne manque pas de goût" (roughly, "no lack of taste"), i.e. NEG(NEG_lex(taste)), the opinion is positive. This property was also observed in (Rowan et al., 2006). Thus, multiple negatives preserving negation concern the following combinations:

NEG_quant(NEG_quant(exp)),
NEG_quant(NEG(exp)),
NEG(NEG_quant(exp)).

We analyse the frequency of our negation categories in a corpus of French opinion texts. We use a manually built subjective lexicon (Benamara et al., 2011) that contains 95 modalities and 21 negations. An analysis of a corpus of 26132 French movie reviews (about 863 TV series) extracted from the allociné web site[1] shows that around 26 % of reviews contain NPIs and/or multiple negations.

3.1 Hypotheses

The effects of each negation type are based on the following hypotheses:

N1.a The negation always reverses the polarity of an opinion expression, that is a positive opinion expression becomes negative when in the scope of a negation. For example, "exceptionnel" ("exceptional") and "pas exceptionnel" ("not exceptional").

N1.b The strength of an opinion expression in the scope of a negation, is not greater than of the opinion expression alone. For example, for the adjective "exceptionnel" ("exceptional"), the strength of its negation, that is "pas exceptionnel" ("not exceptional"), is lower.

N2. The strength of an expression when in the scope of a NEG_quant is greater than when in the scope of a NEG. For instance: "jamais exceptionnel" ("never exceptional") is stronger than "pas exceptionnel" ("not exceptional").

N3. NEG_lex has the same effect as NEG, as for *lack of taste* and *no taste*.

N4. The strength of an expression when in the scope of multiple negatives is greater than when in the scope of each negation alone. For example, "plus jamais bon" ("no longer ever good") is stronger than "plus bon" ("no longer good").

3.2 The experimental setup

The previous hypotheses have been empirically validated by volunteer subjects through two protocols: Protocol 1 for N1.a and N1.b, and Protocol 2 for N2 to N4 [2].

Both protocols are based on a set of questions that we built so that: (1) they reflect the most frequent linguistic structures found in our corpus, and (2) they do not contain words or expressions on which people have prior opinions for/against. In addition, the number of questions within each protocol was designed so that we ensure a trade-off between the amount of data needed for proving our hypotheses and the quality of the data, subjects have to remain focused in order to avoid errors due to tiredness.

Protocol 1. A set of six questions are shown to subjects. In each question, an opinionated sentence is presented, along with its negation using negative operators, as in "This student is brilliant" and "This student is *not* brilliant". The strengths of the opinions vary from one question to another on a discrete scale. Several types of scales have been used in sentiment analysis research, going from continuous scales (Benamara et al., 2007) to discrete ones

[1] http://www.allocine.fr

[2] They are respectively available at: http://goo.gl/CQzKy and http://goo.gl/YnZPS.

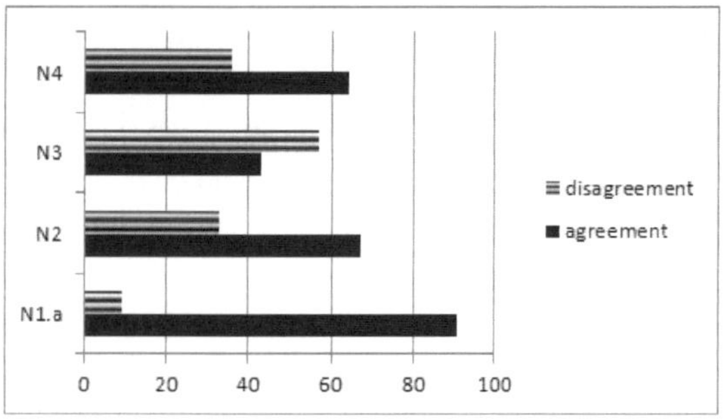

Figure 1: Empirical validation of N1 to N4.

(Taboada et al., 2011). Since our negation hypotheses have to be evaluated against human subjects, the chosen length of the scale has to ensure a trade-off between a fine-grained categorisation of subjective words and the reliability of this categorisation with respect to human judgments. We thus use in our framework a discrete 7-point scale, going from -3 (which corresponds to "extremely negative" opinions) to $+3$ (for "extremely positive" ones) to quantify the strength of an opinion expression. Note that 0 corresponds to cases where in the absence of any context, the opinion expression can be neither positive nor negative. A set of 81 native French speakers were asked to indicate the strength of each sentence in a question on the same 7-point scale.

Protocol 2. Eight questions are shown. Each question contains a pair of sentences: one containing a negative operator, the other having either a negative quantifier or a lexical negation, or multiple negatives, as in "This student is *not* brilliant" and "This student is *never* brilliant". Subjects are asked to compare the strengths of the sentences in each pair. A set of 96 native French speakers participated in this study.

3.3 Results

The results of these assessments are shown in Figure 1, as the average agreement and disagreement between the subjects' answers and our hypotheses. The results show that all four hypotheses are validated. For N1.a, we obtain an average agreement of 90.7 % when excluding the answers corresponding to the strength 0 (20.37 % of all answers). We note that for opinion strengths from -1 to $+2$ (that is, "mildly negative" to "very positive" opinions), N1.a is 100 % verified. The same trend is observed for -2 ("very negative") and $+3$ opinion strengths (87.8 % and 93 % agreement, respectively). However, for "extremely negative" opinions, e.g., "l'acteur est nullisime" ("the actor is worthless"), we observe that only 48.8 % of subjects reverse its polarity. The results for N1.b are shown in Table 1. The rows correspond to opinion strenghts given by subjects for sentences without negation and the columns, and the subjects' answers to the same sentences, this time negated. In this table, we discarded the row for the subjects' answers to the 0-strength original sentences (without negation) because the number of instances was very low.

	+3	+2	+1	0	-1	-2	-3
+3	0	0	4.7	32.9	**58.9**	3.5	0
+2	0	0	0	4.9	**82.0**	13.1	0
+1	0	0	0	0	**84.3**	14.5	1.2
-1	0	0	**62.5**	37.5	0	0	0
-2	0	1.2	**51.9**	39.5	7.4	0	0
-3	0	1.4	26.4	**43.0**	23.6	5.6	0

Table 1: Results (in percents) for N1.b

We observe that the hypothesis N1.b is verified for all configurations of strengths. In addition, a non-negligible percentage of the subjects assign a 0 strength to the negation of all negative opinion expressions. This is particularly salient for extremely negative expressions. The same goes for extremely positive expressions.

N2 is verified at 67 %. This might me because the gap between the strength of `NEG_quant (exp)` and `NEG(exp)` is rather small.

N3 is verified at 43 %. This low result reflects the fact that, as expected, for "lack of" (i.e., "manque de", very frequent in French movie reviews) N3 is not validated: 81 % of the subjects consider the opinion in the scope of this lexical negation to be less negative than the opinion in the scope of the negative operator "not". This disparity in the results show that a thorougher study has to be undertaken in order to better distill the effect of lexical negations on opinion expressions.

Finally, N4 is verified at almost 64 %. The disagreement comes from the question testing the effect of the `NEG_quant (NEG_quant)` combination. We think this might come from the fact that NEG_quant already boosts the strength of an opinion expression, hence adding more NEG_quant does not necessarily yield an even stronger opinion expression.

4 Dealing with Modality

Drawing partly on (Portner, 2009) and on (Larreya, 2004) for French, we have chosen to split modality in three categories:

- *buletic*, denoted by Mod_B – it indicates the speaker's desires/wishes. This type of modality is expressed via a closed set of verbs denoting hope e.g. "I *wish* he were kind".
- *epistemic*, denoted by Mod_E – it indicates the speaker's belief in the propositional content he asserts. It is expressed via doubt, possibility or necessity adverbs, such as "peut-être" ("perhaps"), "décidément" ("definitely"), "certainement" ("certainly"), etc., and via the verbs "devoir" ("have to"), "falloir" ("need to/must") and "pouvoir" ("may/can"), e.g. "The movie *might* be good",
- *deontic*, denoted by Mod_D – it indicates a possibility or an obligation (with their contrapositives, impossibility and permission, respectively). It is only expressed via the same modal verbs as for epistemic modality, but with a deontic reading, e.g., "You *must* go see the movie".

Note that this classification takes into account neither evidential usage of modality nor epistemic modalities expressed in conditional verb moods since these usages are less frequent in our corpus.

Just like for negations, we project these categories on our corpus of French movie reviews and we observe that 53 % of the reviews contain at least one modal construction. In addition, the most frequent modals in those reviews are in decreasing order of occurrence: the epistemic and deontic verbs "devoir" and "pouvoir", buletic modal verbs and epistemic adverbs.

Unlike for negations, for the moment we do not take into account cumulative effects of modalities on an opinion expression, like in: "You *definitely must* see the movie!" as well as combination of negations and modalities.

We consider that each modal expression has a semantic effect on opinions. Unlike negation, this effect is not on both the polarity and the strength of opinions, but only on their *strength* – for instance, the strength of the recommendation "You must go see the movie, it's a blast" is greater than for "Go see the movie, it's a blast", and *certainty degree* – for instance, "This movie is *definitely* good" has a greater certainty than "This movie is good". In our framework, the strength is discretized on a three-level scale, going from 1 (minimal strength) to 3 (maximal strength). The certainty degree also has three possible values, in line with standard literature (Lyons, 1977; Saurí and Pustejovsky, 2009): *possible*, *probable* and *certain*. However, we consider that, in an opinion analysis context, the frontier between the first two values is rather vague, hence we conflate them into a value that we denote by *uncertain*. We thus obtain two certainty degrees, from which we built a three-level scale, by inserting between these values a "default" certainty degree for all expressions which are neither a modal nor in the scope of a modal.

4.1 Hypotheses

We will now specify the semantic effect of each modality type, on the strength and/or certainty degree of the opinion expressions. These effects are structured as a set of six hypotheses:

M1. Mod_B alters the certainty degree of opinion expressions in its scope. Thus, the certainty degree of an opinion expression in the scope of a Mod_B is weaker than the certainty degree of the opinion expression itself. e.g. in "I *hope* this movie is funny" there is less certainty than in "This movie is funny".

M2.1 Mod_E alters the certainty degree of opinion expressions in its scope. For adverbial Mod_E, this degree is altered according to the certainty of the respective adverb: if the latter is uncertain, then the certainty of the opinion in the scope of the adverb is reduced; otherwise, the certainty is augmented. For instance, "Le film est *probablement* bon" ("*Probably* the film is good") is less certain than "Le film est bon" ("The film is good"), which is, in turn, less certain than "Le film est *décidément* bon" ("The film is *definitely* good").

M2.2 The certainty of opinion expressions when in the scope of a verbal `Mod_E` is always lower than when alone. It varies according to the certainty of the respective verb, from *pouvoir* – lowest certainty, to *devoir* and *falloir* – greater certainty. For instance, the certainty of "Le film *peut* être bon" ("the film *might* be good") is lower than of "Le film *doit* être bon" ("the film *must* be good"), which, in turn, is lower than of "Le film est bon" ("the film is good").

M2.3 The certainty degrees of opinion expressions in the scope of epistemic *devoir* and *falloir* are the same.

M3.1 `Mod_D` alters the strength of opinion expressions in its scope. Hence, strength varies according to the verb: *pouvoir* reduces the strength of the opinion, whereas *devoir* and *falloir* boost it.

M3.2 The strengths of opinion expressions in the scope of deontic *devoir* and *falloir* are the same.

4.2 The experimental setup

We empirically validated the previous hypotheses through the same methodology as for negation. We designed three protocols, Protocol 1 for M1, Protocol 2 for M2.1 to M2.3, and Protocol 3 for M3.1 and M3.2.

Protocol 1. In this protocol, five questions are proposed. In one of them, the subject is presented an opinionated sentence without modality. In each of the other questions, we present a subjective sentence with buletic modality. For each question, we then ask the subject to specify whether the author of the sentence has an established opinion (positive or negative), e.g., "I saw this movie yesterday. I *hope* it will be a blockbuster.", or "The movie is interesting.", or hasn't an established opinion yet "I hope this movie is interesting". 78 native French speakers participated in this protocol.

Protocol 2. Eight questions are proposed to subjects. In each question we present an opinionated sentence. The first one is a sentence without modality, e.g. "The movie is good". Each of the other sentences contains an epistemic modality of different certainty degree, either "uncertain" or "certain". 111 native French speakers were asked whether the modal sentence was less, more or as certain as the sentence without modality.

Protocol 3. Four questions are presented. In each question we show a pair of opinionated sentences: one sentence without modality, and another one with a deontic modality, as in "Go see this movie, it is good" and "You *should* go see this movie, it is good". We ask subjects compare the strengths of the sentences in each pair. A set of 78 native French speakers participated in this study.

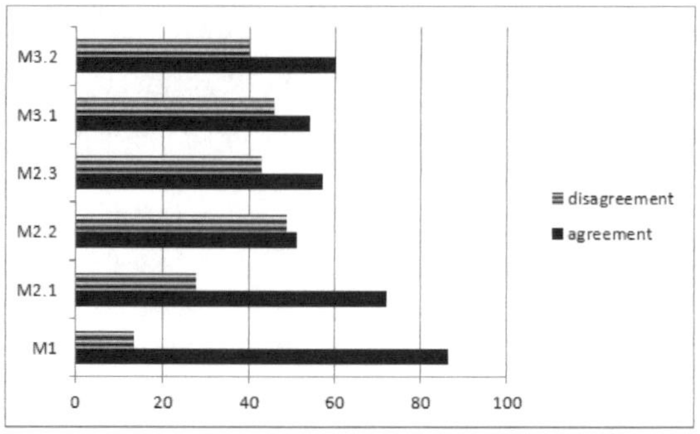

Figure 2: Empirical validation of M1 to M3.2.

4.3 Results

We show the results of these assessments in Figure 2. M1 is validated at 86.5 %. More specifically, when the phrase in the scope of the buletic modality denotes an event, all subjects consider it to vehiculate an opinion. This, in French at least, usually corresponds to an implicit opinion[3]. Moreover, according to all subjects, buletic modality cancels the opinion in its scope, when the phrase expressing the latter denotes a state. Therefore, subjective words do not make sentences like "I hope her husband is kind" opinionated.

M2.1 is validated at around 72 % for both certainty degrees ("certain" and "uncertain"), which shows that, in addition to polarity and strength, certainty is a relevant feature of an opinion expression. Concerning M2.2, almost 79 % of the subjects validated that a phrase when outscoped by "pouvoir" is less certain than when outscoped by "devoir", whereas only 23 % of them consider that "devoir" lowers the certainty degree of the phrase in its scope. M2.3 is validated at around 57 % overall since for "devoir" ("have to") and "falloir" ("need to"/"must") subjects considered them as having the

[3]Implicit opinions, also called opinionated sentences (Liu, 2010), are sentences that express positive or negative opinions and do not contain any explicit subjective clues. Here are some examples: "The movie is not bad, although some persons left the auditorium" or "Laborious and copy/paste of the first part".

same effect.

M3.1 is validated to a lesser extent: 54 %. 62.5 % of the subjects agreed with the hypothesis that deontic "pouvoir" ("may"/"can") reduces the strength of the opinion in its scope. This might be explained by the ambiguity between deontic and epistemic readings of these three verbs. The strengths of "devoir" and "falloir" are deemed identical (M3.2) at 60 %. The rest of 40 % are evenly split between "devoir" being stronger than "falloir" and vice versa.

5 Conclusion

In this paper, we showed that the effects of modality and negation on opinion expressions in their scope depend on the type of these operators. Based on a set of protocols, we empirically validated that negation affects both polarity and strength, and that negative quantifiers and multiple negations boost the strength of the negation. We also empirically validate that modality affects the strength, in case of deontic modality, and the certainty degree for buletic and epistemic modality. Our approach is novel in two ways:

- Our treatment of negation goes beyond the approaches of (Wilson et al., 2009)(Taboada et al., 2011) and (Liu and Seneff, 2009) since we propose a specific treatment for negative polarity items and for multiple negatives. In addition, our results for negative operators confirm, as in (Taboada et al., 2011) and (Liu and Seneff, 2009), that the strength of an opinion expression in the scope of a negation, is not greater than of the opinion expression alone.
- For modality, to our knowledge, our approach is the first study dealing with the semantics of modality for sentiment analysis.

The empirical results reported in this paper provide a basis for future opinion analysis systems that have to compute the sentiment orientation at the sentence or at the clause level.

In further work, we plan to study the effect of cumulative modalities, as in "you definitely must see this movie", and of co-occurring negation and modality, as in " you should not go see this movie", on opinion expressions. We also plan to evaluate to what extent our empirical results extrapolate to other languages. Finally, we will plug our results to a computational model in order to determine the contextual polarity of opinion expressions at the sentence or clause level.

Acknowledgement

This work was supported by a DGA-RAPID project under grant number 0102906143. We also thank all the volunteers for participating in the experiments.

References

Anne Abeillé and Danièle Godard. 2010. The grande grammaire du français project. In *Proceedings of LREC'10.*

Farah Benamara, Carmine Cesarano, Antonio Picariello, Diego Reforgiato, and V. S. Subrahmanian. 2007. Sentiment analysis: Adjectives and adverbs are better than adjectives alone. In *Proceedings of ICWSM.*

Farah Benamara, Baptiste Chardon, Yannick Mathieu, and Vladimir Popescu. 2011. Towards context-based subjectivity analysis. In *Proceedings of 5th International Joint Conference on Natural Language Processing*, pages 1180–1188.

Yejin Choi and Claire Cardie. 2008. Learning with compositional semantics as structural inference for subsentential sentiment analysis. In *Proceedings of EMNLP'08*, pages 793–801.

Francis Corblin and Lucia Tovena. 2003. L'expression de la négation dans les langues romanes. In D. Godard., editor, *Les langues romanes : problèmes de la phrase simple*. Paris: CNRS Editions.

V. Ganter and M. Strube. 2009. Finding hedges by chasing weasels: Hedge detection using wikipedia tags and shallow linguistic features. In *Proceedings of ACL-IJCNLP'09*, pages 173–176.

Anastasia Giannakidou. 2011. Positive polarity items and negative polarity items: variation, licensing, and compositionality. *Semantics: An International Handbook of Natural Language Meaning.*

Danièle Godard. to appear. Les négateurs. In *La Grande Grammaire du français*, chapter 10.

Stephan Greene and Philip Resnik. 2009. More than words: Syntactic packaging and implicit sentiment. In *Proceedings of HLT-NAACL'09*, pages 503–511.

Laurence Horn. 1989. *A natural history of negation.* University of Chicago Press.

Alistair Kennedy and Diana Inkpen. 2006. Sentiment classification of movie and product reviews using contextual valence shifters. *Computational Intelligence*, 22(2):110–125.

Takeshi S. Kobayakawa, Tadashi Kumano, Hideki Tanaka, Naoaki Okazaki, Jin-Dong Kim, and Jun ichi Tsujii. 2009. Opinion classification with tree kernel svm using linguistic modality analysis. In *Proceedings of CIKM'09*, pages 1791–1794.

Paul Larreya. 2004. L'expression de la modalité en français et en anglais (domaine verbal). *Revue belge de philologie et d'histoire*, 82(3):733–762.

Jingjing Liu and Stephanie Seneff. 2009. Review sentiment scoring via a parse-and-paraphrase paradigm. In *Proceedings of EMNLP'09*, pages 161–169.

Bing Liu. 2010. Sentiment analysis and subjectivity. In Nitin Indurkhya and Fred J. Damerau, editors, *Handbook of Natural Language Processing, Second Edition*. CRC Press, Taylor and Francis Group, Boca Raton, FL.

J. Lyons. 1977. *Semantics. vol. 2*. Cambridge University Press.

Jacques Moeschler. 1992. The pragmatic aspects of linguistic negation: Speech act, argumentation and pragmatic inference. *Argumentation*, 6(1):51–76.

Karo Moilanen and Stephen Pulman. 2007. Sentiment composition. In *Proceedings of RANLP'07*, pages 378–382.

Claude Muller. 1991. *La négation en français. Syntaxe, sémantique et éléments de comparaison avec les autres langues romanes:*. Droz, Genève.

Livia Polanyi and Annie Zaenen. 2006. Contextual valence shifters. In *Computing Attitude and Affect in Text: Theory and Applications*, The Information Retrieval Series, pages 1–10. Springer-Verlag.

Paul Portner. 2009. *Modality*, volume 1. Oxford University Press, USA.

Nairn Rowan, Cleo Condoravdi, and Lauri Karttunen. 2006. Computing relative polarity for textual inference. In *Proceedings of ICoS-5*.

Victoria Rubin. 2010. Epistemic modality: From uncertainty to certainty in the context of information seeking as interactions with texts. *Information Processing and Management*, 46(5):533–540.

Roser Saurí and James Pustejovsky. 2009. FactBank: a corpus annotated with event factuality. *Language Resources and Evaluation*, 43(3):227–268.

Henriette De Swart. 2010. Expression and interpretation of negation. An OT typology. *Studies in Natural Language and Linguistic Theory*, 77.

Maite Taboada, Julian Brooke, Milan Tofiloski, Kimberly Voll, and Manfred Stede. 2011. Lexicon-based methods for sentiment analysis. *Computational Linguistics*, 37:267–307.

V. Vincze, G. Szarvas, R. Farkas, G. Móra, and J. Csirik. 2008. The bioscope corpus: biomedical texts annotated for uncertainty, negation and their scopes. *BMC bioinformatics*, 9(Suppl 11):S9.

Michael Wiegand, Alexandra Balahur, Benjamin Roth, Dietrich Klakow, and Andrés Montoyo. 2010. A survey on the role of negation in sentiment analysis. In *Proceedings of the Workshop on Negation and Speculation in Natural Language Processing*, pages 60–68.

Theresa Wilson, Janyce Wiebe, and Paul Hoffmann. 2005. Recognizing contextual polarity in phrase-level sentiment analysis. In *Proceedings of HLT'05*, pages 347–354.

Theresa Wilson, Janyce Wiebe, and Paul Hoffmann. 2009. Recognizing contextual polarity: An exploration of features for phrase-level sentiment analysis. *Computational Linguistics*, 35(3):399–433.

Ainur Yessenalina and Claire Cardie. 2011. Compositional matrix-space models for sentiment analysis. In *Proceedings of EMNLP'11*, pages 172–182.

Q. Zhao, C. Sun, B. Liu, and Y. Cheng. 2010. Learning to detect hedges and their scope using crf. In *Proceedings of CoNLL'10*, pages 100–105.

Linking Uncertainty in Physicians' Narratives to Diagnostic Correctness

Wilson McCoy
Department of Interactive Games and Media
wgm4143@rit.edu

Cecilia Ovesdotter Alm
Department of English
coagla@rit.edu

Cara Calvelli
College of Health Sciences and Technology
cfcscl@rit.edu

Jeff B. Pelz
Center for Imaging Science
pelz@cis.rit.edu

Pengcheng Shi
Computing and Information Sciences
pengcheng.shi@rit.edu

Anne Haake
Computing and Information Sciences
anne.haake@rit.edu

Rochester Institute of Technology

Abstract

In the medical domain, misdiagnoses and diagnostic uncertainty put lives at risk and incur substantial financial costs. Clearly, medical reasoning and decision-making need to be better understood. We explore a possible link between linguistic expression and diagnostic correctness. We report on an unusual data set of spoken diagnostic narratives used to computationally model and predict diagnostic correctness based on automatically extracted and linguistically motivated features that capture physicians' uncertainty. A multimodal data set was collected as dermatologists viewed images of skin conditions and explained their diagnostic process and observations aloud. We discuss experimentation and analysis in initial and secondary pilot studies. In both cases, we experimented with computational modeling using features from the acoustic-prosodic and lexical-structural linguistic modalities.

1 Introduction

Up to 20% of post-mortem diagnoses in the United States are inconsistent with the diagnosis before death (Graber, 2005). These misdiagnoses cost both human lives and estimated millions of dollars every year. To find where and why misdiagnoses occur, it is necessary to improve our understanding of doctors' diagnostic reasoning and how it is linked to diagnostic uncertainty and correctness. Our contribution begins to explore the computational modeling of this phenomenon in diagnostic narratives. From a cognitive science perspective, we are contributing to the research on medical reasoning and how it is linguistically expressed. In the long term, this area of work could be a useful decision-making component for flagging diagnoses that need further review.

The study used an unusual multimodal data set collected in a modified Master-Apprentice interaction scenario. It comprises both gaze and linguistic data. The present study focuses on the linguistic data which in turn can be conceptualized as consisting of both acoustic-prosodic and lexical-structural modalities. This data set can further be used to link vision and language research to understand human cognition in expert decision-making scenarios.

We report on a study conducted in two phases. First, an initial pilot study involved a preliminary annotation of a small subset of the collected diagnostic narratives and also investigated the prediction of diagnostic correctness using a set of linguistic features from speech recordings and their verbal transcriptions. This provided initial features relevant to classification, helped us identify annotation issues, and gave us insight on how to improve the annotation scheme used for annotating ground truth data. Next, a second pilot study was performed, building on what was learned in the initial pilot study. The second pilot study involved a larger data set with a revised and improved annotation scheme that considered gradient correctness at different steps of the diagnostic reasoning process: (1) medical lesion morphology (e.g. recognizing the lesion type as a scaly erythematous plaque), (2) differential diagnosis (i.e. providing a set of possible final diagnoses), and (3) final diagnosis (e.g. identifying the disease condition as psoriasis). We also experiment with classification using an expanded feature set motivated by the initial pilot study and by previously published research. We report on results that consider different algorithms, feature set modalities, diagnostic reasoning steps, and coarse vs. fine grained classes as explained below in Section 4.3.

2 Previous Work

Much work has been done in the area of medical decision-making. Pelaccia et al. (2011) have viewed clinical reasoning through the lens of dual-process theory. They posit that two systems are at work in the mind of a clinician: the *intuitive* system which quickly produces a response based on experience and a holistic view of the situation, versus the *analytic* system which slowly and logically steps through the problem with conscious use of knowledge. Croskerry (2009) stated that "[i]f the presentation is not recognized, or if it is unduly ambiguous or there is uncertainty, [analytic] processes engage instead" (p. 1022); for instance, if a clinician is unfamiliar with a disease or unsure of their intuitive answer. We assume that different reasoning systems may cause changes in linguistic behaviors. For example, when engaging the slower analytic system, it seems reasonable that frequent pausing could appear as an indication of, e.g., uncertainty or thoughtfulness.

Several studies have explored the task of detecting uncertainty through language. Uncertainty detection necessitates inference of extra-propositional meaning and is arguably a subjective natural language problem, i.e. part of a family of problems that are increasingly receiving attention in computational linguistics. These problems involve more dynamic classification targets and different performance expectations (Alm, 2011). Pon-Barry and Shieber (2009) have shown encouraging results in finding uncertainty using acoustic-prosodic features at the word, word's local context, and whole utterance levels. Henriksson and Velupillai (2010) used "speculative words" (e.g., *could, generally, should, may, sort of*, etc.) as well as "certainty amplifiers" (e.g., *definitely, positively, must*, etc.) to determine uncertainty in text. Velupillai (2010) also applied the same approach to medical texts and noted that acoustic-prosodic features should be considered alongside salient lexical-structural features as indicators of uncertainty. In this work, we draw on the insight of such previous work, but we also extend the types of linguistic evidence considered for identifying possible links to diagnostic correctness.

As another type of linguistic evidence, disfluencies make up potentially important linguistic evidence. Zwarts and Johnson (2011) found that the occurrence of disfluencies that had been removed could be predicted to a satisfactory degree. Pakhomov (1999) observed that such disfluencies are just as common in monologues as in dialogues even though there is no need for the speakers to indicate that they wish to continue speaking. This finding is important for the work presented here because our modified use of the Master-Apprentice scenario results in a particular dialogic interaction with the listener remaining silent. Perhaps most importantly, Clark and Fox Tree (2002) postulated that filled pauses (e.g., *um, uh, er*, etc.) play a meaningful role in speech. For example, they may signal that the speaker is yet to finish speaking or searching for a word. There is some controversy about this claim, however, as explained by Corley and Stewart (2008). The scholarly controversy about the role of disfluencies indicates that more research is needed to understand the disfluency phenomenon, including how it relates to extra-propositional meaning.

3 Data Set

The original elicitation experiment included 16 physicians with dermatological expertise. Of these, 12 were attending physicians and 4 were residents (i.e. dermatologists in training). The observers were shown a series of 50 images of dermatological conditions. The summary of this collected data is shown in Table 1, with reference to the pilot studies.

The physicians were instructed to narrate, in English, their thoughts and observations about each image to a student, who remained silent, as they arrived at a differential diagnosis or a possible final diagnosis. This data elicitation approach is a modified version of the Master-Apprentice interaction scenario (Beyer and Holtzblatt, 1997). This elicitation setup is shown in Figure 1. It allows us to extract information about the Master's (i.e. in this case, the physician's) cognitive process by coaxing them to

Data parameters	Quantity
# of participating doctors	16
# of images for which narratives were collected	50
# of time-aligned narratives in the initial pilot study	160
# of time-aligned narratives in the second pilot study	707

Table 1: This table summarizes the data. Of the collected narratives, 707 are included in this work; audio is unavailable for some narratives.

vocalize their thoughts in rich detail. This teaching-oriented scenario really is a monologue, yet induces a feeling of dialogic interaction in the Master.

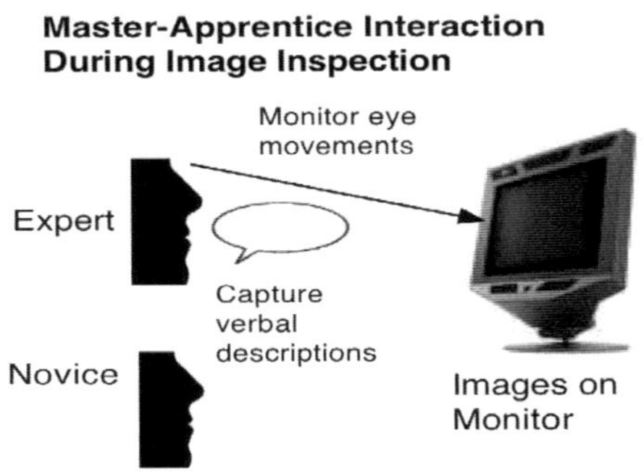

Figure 1: The Master-Apprentice interaction scenario allows us to extract information about the Master's (here: doctor's) cognitive processes.

The form of narratives collected can be analyzed in many ways. Figure 2 shows two narratives, recently elicited and similar to the ones in the study's data set, that are used here with permission as examples. In terms of diagnostic reasoning styles, referring to Pelaccia et al. (2011), we can propose that observer A may be using the *intuitive* system and that observer B may be using the *analytical* system. Observer A does not provide a differential diagnosis and jumps straight to his/her final diagnosis, which in this case is correct. We can postulate that observer A looks at the general area of the lesion and uses previous experience or heuristic knowledge to come to the correct diagnosis. This presumed use of the *intuitive* system could potentially relate to the depth of previous experience with a disease, for example. Observer B, on the other hand, might be using the *analytical* system. Observer B steps through the diagnosis in a methodical process and uses evidence presented to rationalize the choice of final diagnosis. Observer B also provides a differential diagnosis unlike observer A. This suggests that observer B is taking advantage of a process of elimination to decide on a final diagnosis.

A. This patient has a pinkish papule with surrounding hypopigmentation in a field of other cherry hemagiomas and nevoid type lesions. The only diagnosis that comes to mind to me is Sutton's nevus.

B. I think I'm looking at an abdomen, possibly. I see a hypopigmented oval-shaped patch in the center of the image. I see that there are two brown macules as well. In the center of the hypopigmented oval patch there appears to be an area that may be a pink macule. Differential diagnosis includes halo nevus, melanoma, post-inflammatory hypopigmentation. I favor a diagnosis of maybe post-inflammatory hypopigmentation.

Figure 2: Two narratives collected in a recent elicitation setup and used here with permission. Narratives A and B are not part of the studied data set, but exemplify data set narratives which could not be distributed. Observers A and B are both looking at an image of a halo or Sutton's nevus as seen in Figure 3. Disfluencies are considered in the experimental work but have been removed for readability in these examples.

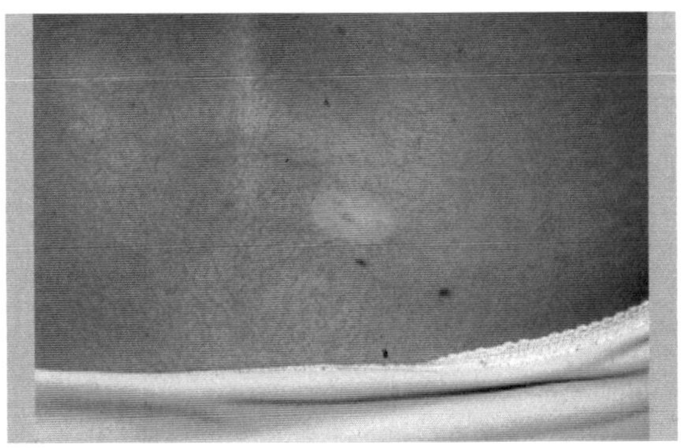

Figure 3: The image of a halo or Sutton's nevus viewed by the observers and the subject of example narratives.

Another way to evaluate these narratives is in terms of correctness and the related concept of diagnostic completeness. Whereas these newly elicited narrative examples have not been annotated by doctors, some observations can still be made. From the point of view of final diagnosis, observer A is correct, unlike observer B. Assessment of diagnostic correctness and completeness can also be made on intermediate steps in the diagnostic process (e.g. differential diagnoses or medical lesion morphological description). Including such steps in the diagnostic process is considered good practice. Observer A does not supply a differential diagnosis and instead skips to the final diagnosis. Observer B provides the correct answer in the differential diagnosis but gives the incorrect final diagnosis. Observer B fully describes the medical lesion morphology presented. Observer A, however, only describes the pink lesion and does not discuss the other two brown lesions.

The speech of the diagnostic narratives was recorded. At the same time, the observers' eye-movements were tracked; the eye-tracking data are considered in another report (Li et al., 2010). We leave the integration of the linguistic and eye-tracking data for future work.

After the collection of the raw audio data, the utterances were manually transcribed and time-aligned at the word level with the speech analysis tool Praat (Boersma, 2001).[1] A sample of the transcription process output is shown in Figure 4. Given our experimental context, off-the-shelf automatic speech recognizers could not transcribe the narratives to the desired quality and resources were not available to create our own automatic transcriber. Manual transcription also preserved disfluencies, which we believe convey meaningful information. Disfluencies were transcribed to include filled pauses (e.g. *uh, um*), false starts (e.g. *pur-reddish purple*), repetitions, and click sounds.

[1]See `http://www.fon.hum.uva.nl/praat/`.

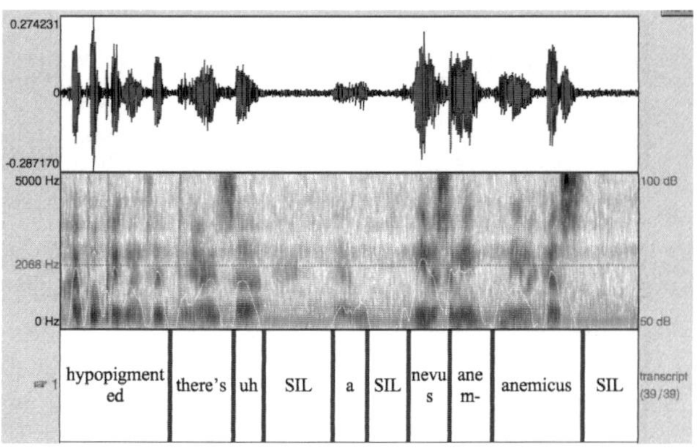

Figure 4: Transcripts were time-aligned in Praat which was also used to extract acoustic-prosodic features.

This study is strengthened by its involvement of medical experts. Trained dermatologists were recruited in the original elicitation experiment as well as the creation and application of both annotation schemes. This is crucial in a knowledge-rich domain such as medicine because the annotation scheme must reflect the domain knowledge. Another study reports on annotation details (McCoy et al., Forthcoming 2012).

4 Classification Study

This section discusses the classification work, first explaining the methodology for the initial pilot study followed by interpretation of results. Next, the methodology of the second pilot study is described.

4.1 Generic Model Overview

This work applies computational modeling designed to predict diagnostic correctness in physicians' narratives based on linguistic features from the acoustic-prosodic and lexical-structural modalities of language, shown in Table 2. Some tests discussed in 4.2 and 4.3 were performed with these modalities separated. These features are inspired by previous work conducted by Szarvas (2008), Szarvas et al. (2008), Litman et al. (2009), Liscombe et al. (2005), and Su et al. (2010).

We can formally express the created model in the following way: Let n_i be an instance in a set of narratives N, let j be a classification method, and let l_i be a label in a set of class labels L. We want to establish a function $f(n_i, j) : l_i$ where l_i is the label assigned to the narrative based on linguistic features from a set F, where $F = f_1, f_2, ...f_k$, as described in Table 2. The baseline for each classifier is defined as the majority class ratio. Using scripts in Praat (Boersma, 2001), Python, and NLTK (Bird et al., 2009), we automatically extracted features for each narrative. Each narrative was annotated with multiple labels relating to its diagnostic correctness. The labeling schemes used in the initial and second pilot studies, respectively, are described in subsections 4.2 and 4.3.

4.2 Initial Pilot Study

The initial pilot classification study allowed the opportunity to refine the prediction target annotation scheme, as well as to explore a preliminary set of linguistic features. 160 narratives were assigned labels of *correct* or *incorrect* for two steps of the diagnostic process: *diagnostic category* and *final diagnosis*. These annotations were done by a dermatologist who did not participate in the elicitation study (co-author Cara Calvelli). For final diagnosis, 70% were marked as correct, and for diagnostic category, 80% were marked as correct. An outcome of the annotation study was learning that the initial annotation scheme needed to be refined. For example, *diagnostic category* had a fuzzy interpretation, and correctness and completeness of diagnoses are found along a gradient in medicine. This led us to pursue an improved annotation scheme with new class labels in the second pilot study, as well as the adoption of a gradient scale of correctness.

Linguistic Modality	Feature at the narrative level
Acoustic-prosodic	Total duration
	Percent silence
	Time silent
	# of silences *
	Time speaking
	# of utterances *
	Initial silence length
	F0 mean (avg. pitch) ○
	F0 min (min. pitch) ○
	F0 max (max. pitch) ○
	dB mean (avg. intensity) ○
	dB max (max. intensity) ○
Lexical-structural	# of words
	words per minute
	# of disfluencies •
	# of certainty amplifiers * •
	# of speculative words * •
	# of stop words * •
	# of content words * •
	# of negations * •
	# of nouns •
	# of verbs •
	# of adjectives •
	# of adverbs •
	Unigram of tokens
	Bigram of tokens
	Trigram of tokens

Table 2: Features used by their respective modalities. Features marked with a * were only included in the second pilot study. Features marked with ○ were included twice; once as their raw value and again as a z-score normalized to its speaker's data in the training set. Features marked with • were also included twice; once as their raw count and again as their value divided by the total number of words in that narrative. Disfluencies were considered as words towards the total word count, silences were not. No feature selection was applied.

For the initial pilot study, basic features were extracted from the diagnostic narratives in two modalities: acoustic-prosodic and lexical-structural (see Table 2). To understand the fundamental aspects of the problem, the initial pilot study experimented with the linguistic modalities separately and together, using three foundational algorithms, as implemented in NLTK (Naive Bayes, Maximum Entropy, Decision Tree), and a maximum vote classifier based on majority consensus of the three basic classifiers. The majority class baselines were 70% for diagnosis and 80% for diagnostic category. The small pilot data set was split into an 80% training set and a 20% testing set. The following results were obtained with the maximum vote classifier.

Utilizing only acoustic-prosodic features, the maximum vote classifier performed 5% above the baseline when testing final diagnosis and 6% below it for diagnostic category. *F0 min* and *initial silence length* appeared as important features. This initial silence length could signal that the observers are able to glean more information from the image, and using this information, they can make a more accurate diagnosis.

Utilizing only lexical-structural features, the model performed near the baseline (+1%) for final diagnosis and 9% better than the baseline for diagnostic category. When combining acoustic-prosodic and lexical-structural modalities, the majority vote classifier performed above the baseline by 5% for final diagnosis and 9% for diagnostic category. We are cautious in our interpretation of these findings. For example, the small size of the data set and the particulars of the data split may have guided the results, and the concept of diagnostic category turned out to be fuzzy and problematic. Nevertheless, the study helped us refine our approach for the second pilot study and redefine the annotation scheme.

4.3 Second Pilot Study

For the second pilot study, we hoped to gain further insight into primarily two questions: (1) How accurately do the tested models perform on three steps of the diagnostic process, and what might influence the performance? (2) In our study scenario, is a certain linguistic modality more important for the classification problem?

The annotation scheme was revised according to findings from the initial pilot study. These revisions were guided by dermatologist and co-author Cara Calvelli. The initial pilot study scheme only annotated for *diagnostic category* and *final diagnosis*. We realized that *diagnostic category* was too slippery of a concept, prone to misunderstanding, to be useful. Instead, we replaced it with two new and more explicit parts of the diagnostic process: medical lesion *morphology* and *differential diagnosis*.

For *final diagnosis*, the class label options of *correct* and *incorrect* could not characterize narratives in which observers had not provided a final diagnosis. Therefore, a third class label of *none* was added. New class labels were also created that corresponded to the diagnostic steps of medical lesion *morphology* and *differential diagnosis*. Medical lesion *morphology*, which is often descriptively complex, allowed the label options *correct*, *incorrect*, and *none*, as well as *correct but incomplete* to deal with correct but under-described medical morphologies. *Differential diagnosis* considered whether or not the final diagnosis appeared in the differential and thus involved the labels *yes*, *no*, and *no differential given*. Table 3 summarizes the refined annotation scheme.

The examples in Figure 2 above can now be analyzed according to the new annotation scheme. Observer A has a *final diagnosis* which should be labeled as *correct* but does not give a differential diagnosis, so the *differential diagnosis* label should be *no differential given*. Observer A also misses parts of the morphological description so the assigned *medical lesion morphology* would likely be *correct but incomplete*. Observer B provides what seems to be a full morphological description as well as lists the correct final diagnosis in the differential diagnosis, yet is incorrect regarding *final diagnosis*. This narrative's labels for medical lesion *morphology* and *differential diagnosis* would most likely be *correct* and *yes* respectively. Further refinements may turn out useful as the data set expands.

Diagnostic step	Possible labels	Count	Ratio
Medical Lesion *Morphology*	*Correct*	537	.83
	Incorrect	36	.06
	None Given	40	.06
	Incomplete	32	.05
Differential Diagnosis	*Yes*	167	.24
	No	101	.14
	No Differential	434	.62
Final Diagnosis	*Correct*	428	.62
	Incorrect	229	.33
	None Given	35	.05

Table 3: Labels for various steps of the diagnostic process as well as their count and ratios of the total narratives, after eliminating those with no annotator agreement. These labels are explained in section 4.3.

Three dermatologists annotated the narratives, assigning a label of correctness for each step in the diagnostic process for a given narrative. Table 3 shows the ratios of labels in the collected annotations. Medical lesion *morphology* is largely correct with only smaller ratios being assigned to other categories. Secondly, a large ratio of narratives were assigned *no differential given* but of those that did provide a differential diagnosis, the correct final diagnosis was more likely to be included than not. Regarding *final diagnosis*, a label of *correct* was most often assigned and few narratives did not provide any *final diagnosis*. These class imbalances, existing at each level, indicated that the smaller classes with fewer instances would be quite challenging for a computational classifier to learn.

Any narrative for which there was not agreement for at least 2 of the 3 dermatologists in a diagnostic step was discarded from the set of narratives considered in that diagnostic step.[2]

[2]Because narratives with disagreement were removed, the total numbers of narratives in the experiment sets differ slightly on the various step of the diagnostic process.

Comparing classification in terms of algorithms, diagnostic steps, and individual classes

Weka (Witten and Frank, 2005)[3] was used with four classification algorithms, which have a widely accepted use in computational linguistics.[4]

Standard performance measures were used to evaluate the classifiers. Both acoustic-prosodic and lexical-structural features were used in a leave-one-out cross-validation scenario, given the small size of the data set. The results are shown in Table 4. Accuracy is considered in relation to the majority class baseline in each case. With this in mind, the high accuracies found when testing medical lesion *morphology* are caused by a large class imbalance. *Differential diagnosis*' best result is 5% more accurate than its baseline while *final diagnosis* and medical lesion *morphology* are closer to their baselines.

	Final Dx	*Diff. Dx*	M. L. *M.*
Baseline	*.62*	*.62*	*.83*
C4.5	.57	.62	.77
SVM	.63	.67	.83
Naive Bayes	.55	.61	.51
Log Regression	.53	.64	.66

Table 4: Accuracy ratios of four algorithms (implemented in Weka) as well as diagnostic steps' majority class baselines. Experiments used algorithms' default parameters for *final diagnosis* (3 labels), *differential diagnosis* (3 labels), and medical lesion *morphology* (4 labels) using leave-one-out cross-validation.

In all scenarios, the SVM algorithm reached or exceeded the majority class baseline. For this reason, other experiments used SVM. The results for the SVM algorithm when considering precision and recall for each class label, at each diagnostic step, are shown in Table 5. Precision is calculated as the number of true positives for a given class divided by the number of narratives classified as the given class. Recall is calculated as the number of true positives for a given class divided by the number of narratives belonging to the given class. As Table 5 shows, and as expected, labels representing large proportions were better identified than labels representing

[3]See http://www.cs.waikato.ac.nz/ml/weka/.

[4]In this initial experimentation, not all features used were independent, although this is not ideal for some algorithms.

Dx step	Labels	Precision	Recall
Medical Lesion *Morphology*	*Correct*	.83	.99
	Incorrect	0	0
	None Given	0	0
	Incomplete	0	0
Differential Diagnosis	*Yes*	.49	.44
	No	.26	.10
	No Diff.	.76	.89
Final Diagnosis	*Correct*	.67	.84
	Incorrect	.32	.47
	None Given	0	0

Table 5: Precision and recall of class labels. These were obtained using the Weka SVM algorithm with default parameters using leave-one-out cross-validation. These correspond to the experiment for SVM in Table 4.

	Final Diagnosis	*Diff. Diagnosis*
Baseline	*.62*	*.62*
Lex.-struct.	.62	.67
Acous.-pros.	.65	.62
All	.63	.67

Table 6: Accuracy ratios for various modalities. Tests were performed for *final diagnosis* and *differential diagnosis* tags with Weka's SVM algorithm using a leave-out-out cross-validation method. Lexical-structural and acoustic-prosodic cases used *only* features in their respective set.

intermediate proportions, and classes with few instances did poorly.

Experimentation with types of feature

To test if one linguistic modality was more important for classification, experiments were run in each of three different ways: with only lexical-structural features, with only acoustic-prosodic features, and with all features. We considered the *final diagnosis* and *differential diagnosis* scenarios. It was decided not to run this experiment in terms of medical lesion *morphology* because of its extreme class imbalance with a high baseline of 83%. Medical lesion *morphology* also differs in being a descriptive step unlike the other two which are more like conclusions. Again, a leave-one-out cross-validation method was used. The results are shown in Table 6.

These results show that, regarding *final diagnosis*, considering only acoustic-prosodic features seemed to yield somewhat higher accuracy than when features were combined. This might reflect that, conceptually, *final diagnosis* captures a global end step in the decision-making process, and we extracted voice features at a global level (across the narrative). In the case of *differential diagnosis*, the lexical-structural features performed best, matching the accuracy of the combined feature set (5% over the majority class baseline). Future study could determine which individual features in these sets were most important.

Experiments with alternative label groupings for some diagnostic steps

Another set of experiments examined performance for adjusted label combinations. To learn more about the model, experiments were run in which selected classes were combined or only certain classes were considered. The class proportions thus changed due to the combinations and/or removal of classes. This was done utilizing all features, the Weka SVM algorithm, and a leave-one-out methodology. Only logically relevant tests that increased class balance are reported here.[5]

An experiment was run on the *differential diagnosis* step. The *no differential given* label was ignored to allow the binary classification of narratives that included differential diagnoses. The new majority class baseline for this test was 62% and this classification performed 1% over its baseline. A similar experiment was run on the *final diagnosis* diagnostic step. Class labels of *incorrect* and *none given* were combined to form binary set of class labels with a 62% baseline. This classification performed 6% over the baseline, i.e., slightly improved performance compared to the scenario with three class labels.

5 Conclusion

In these pilot studies, initial insight has been gained regarding the computational linguistic modeling of extra-propositional meaning but we acknowledge that these results need to be confirmed with new data.

This paper extracted features, which could possibly relate to uncertainty, at the global level of a narrative to classify correctness of three diagnostic reasoning steps. These steps are in essence local phenomena and a better understanding of how uncertainty is locally expressed in the diagnostic process is needed. Also, this work does not consider parametrization of algorithms or the role of feature selection. In future work, by considering only the features that are most important, a better understanding of linguistic expression in relation to diagnostic correctness could be achieved, and likely result in better performing models. One possible future adaptation would be the utilization of the Unified Medical Language System to improve the lexical features used Woods et al. (2006).

Other future work includes integrating eye movement data into prediction models. The gaze modality informs us as to where the observers were looking when they were verbalizing their diagnostic process. We can thus map the narratives to how gaze was positioned on an image. Behavioral indicators of doctors' diagnostic reasoning likely extend beyond language. By integrating gaze and linguistic information, much could be learned regarding perceptual and conceptual knowledge.

Through this study, we have moved towards understanding reasoning in medical narratives, and we have come one step closer to linking the spoken words of doctors to their cognitive processes. In a much more refined, future form, certainty or correctness detection could become useful to help understanding medical reasoning or help guide medical reasoning or detect misdiagnosis.

[5]Other experiments were run but are not reported because they have no use in future implementations.

Acknowledgements

This research supported by NIH 1 R21 LM010039-01A1, NSF IIS-0941452, RIT GCCIS Seed Funding, and RIT Research Computing (http://rc.rit.edu). We would like to thank Lowell A. Goldsmith, M.D. and the anonymous reviewers for their comments.

References

Cecilia Ovesdotter Alm. 2011. Subjective Natural Language Problems: Motivations, Applications, Characterizations, and Implications. *Proceedings of the 49th Annual Meeting of the Association for Computational Linguistics*, pages 107–112.

Hugh Beyer and Karen Holtzblatt. 1997. *Contextual Design: Defining Customer-Centered Systems*. Morgan Kaufmann.

Steven Bird, Ewan Klein, and Edward Loper. 2009. *Natural Language Processing with Python*. O'Reilly Media.

Paul Boersma. 2001. Praat, a system for doing phonetics by computer. *Glot International*, pages 341–345.

Herbert Clark and Jean Fox Tree. 2002. Using uh and um in spontaneous speaking. *Cognition*, pages 73–111.

Martin Corley and Oliver Stewart. 2008. Hesitation disfluencies in spontaneous speech: The meaning of um. *Language and Linguistics Compass*, 5(2):589–602.

Pat Croskerry. 2009. A universal model of diagnostic reasoning. *Academic Medicine*, pages 1022–1028.

Mark Graber. 2005. Diagnostic errors in medicine: A case of neglect. *The Joint Commission Journal on Quality and Patient Safety*, pages 106–113.

Aron Henriksson and Sumithra Velupillai. 2010. Levels of certainty in knowledge-intensive corpora: An initial annotation study. *Proceedings of the Workshop on Negation and Speculation in Natural Language Processing*, pages 41–45.

Rui Li, Preethi Vaidyanathan, Sai Mulpuru, Jeff Pelz, Pengcheng Shi, Cara Calvelli, and Anne Haake. 2010. Human-centric approaches to image understanding and retrieval. *Image Processing Workshop, Western New York*, pages 62–65.

Jackson Liscombe, Julia Hirschberg, and Jennifer Venditti. 2005. Detecting certainness in spoken tutorial dialogues. *Proceedings of Interspeech*, pages 1837–1840.

Diane Litman, Mihail Rotaru, and Greg Nicholas. 2009. Classifying turn-level uncertainty using word-level prosody. *Proceedings of Interspeech*, pages 2003–2006.

Wilson McCoy, Cecilia Ovesdotter Alm, Cara Calvelli, Rui Li, Jeff Pelz, Pengcheng Shi, and Anne Haake. Forthcoming-2012. Annotation schemes to encode domain knowledge in medical narratives. *Proceedings of the Sixth Linguistic Annotation Workshop*.

Sergey Pakhomov. 1999. Modeling filled pauses in medical dictations. *Proceedings of the 37th Annual Meeting of the Association for Computational Linguistics on Computational Linguistics*, pages 619–624.

Thierry Pelaccia, Jacques Tardif, Emmanuel Triby, and Bernard Charlin. 2011. An analysis of clinical reasoning through a recent and comprehensive approach: the dual-process theory. *Medical Education Online*, 16:5890.

Heather Pon-Barry and Stuart Shieber. 2009. The importance of sub-utterance prosody in predicting level of certainty. *Proceedings of NAACL HLT*, pages 105–108.

Qi Su, Chu-Ren Huang, and Helen Kai-yun Chen. 2010. Evidentiality for text trustworthiness detection. *Proceedings of the 2010 Workshop on NLP and Linguistics: Finding the Common Ground ACL 2010*, pages 10–17.

Gyorgy Szarvas, Veronika Vincze, Richard Farkas, and Janos Csirik. 2008. The bioscope corpus: annotation for negation, uncertainty and their scope in biomedical texts. *BioNLP 2008: Current Trends in Biomedical Natural Language Processing*, pages 38–45.

Gyorgy Szarvas. 2008. Hedge classification in biomedical texts with a weakly supervised selection of keywords. *Proceedings of 46th Annual Meeting of the Association of Computational Linguistics*, pages 281–289.

Sumithra Velupillai. 2010. Towards a better understanding of uncertainties and speculations in Swedish clinical text - analysis of an initial annotation trial. *Proceedings of the Workshop on Negation and Speculation in Natural Language Processing*, pages 14–22.

Ian H. Witten and Eibe Frank. 2005. *Data Mining: Practical Machine Learning Tools and Techniques*. Morgan Kaufmann.

James Woods, Charles Sneiderman, Karam Hameed, Michael Ackerman, and Charlie Hatton. 2006. Using umls metathesaurus concepts to describe medical images: dermatology vocabulary. *Computers in Biology and Medicine 36*, pages 89–100.

Simon Zwarts and Mark Johnson. 2011. The impact of language models and loss functions on repair disfluency detection. *Proceedings of the 49th Annual Meeting of the Association for Computational Linguistics*, pages 703–711.

Factuality Detection on the Cheap: Inferring Factuality for Increased Precision in Detecting Negated Events

Erik Velldal
University of Oslo
Department of Informatics
erikve@ifi.uio.no

Jonathon Read
University of Oslo
Department of Informatics
jread@ifi.uio.no

Abstract

This paper describes a system for discriminating between factual and non-factual contexts, trained on weakly labeled data by taking advantage of information implicit in annotations of negated events. In addition to evaluating factuality detection in isolation, we also evaluate its impact on a system for event detection. The two components for factuality detection and event detection form part of a system for identifying negative factual events, or counterfacts, with top-ranked results in the *SEM 2012 shared task.

1 Introduction

The First Joint Conference on Lexical and Computational Semantics (*SEM 2012) is hosting a shared task[1] (Morante and Blanco, 2012) on identifying various elements of negation, and one of the subtasks is to identify negated *events*. However, only events occurring in *factual statements* should be labeled. This paper describes pilot experiments on how to train a *factuality classifier* by taking advantage of implicit information on factuality in annotations of negation. In addition to evaluating factuality detection in isolation, we also assess its impact when embedded in a system for *event detection*. The system was ranked first for the *SEM 2012 subtask of identifying negated events, and also formed part of the top-ranked system in the shared task overall (Read et al., 2012). The experiments presented in this paper further improves on these initial results.

[1]The web site of the 2012 *SEM Shared Task: `http://www.clips.ua.ac.be/sem2012-st-neg/`

Note that the system was designed for submission to the closed track of the shared task, which means development is constrained to using the data provided by the task organizers.

The rest of the paper is structured as follows. We start in Section 2 by giving a brief overview of related work and resources. In Section 3 we then present the problem statement in more detail, along with the relevant data sets. This section also discusses the notion of (non-)factuality assumed in the current paper. We then go on to present and evaluate the factuality classifier in Section 4. In Section 5 we move on to describe the event detection task, which is handled by learning a discriminative ranking function over candidate tokens within the negation scope, using features from paths in constituent trees. Both the event ranking function and the factuality classifier are implemented using the Support Vector Machine (SVM) framework. After evaluating the impact of factuality detection on event detection, we finally provide some concluding remarks and discussion of future directions in Section 6.

2 Related Work

Note that the *SEM 2012 shared task singled out three separate subtasks for the problem of recognizing negation, namely the identification of negation *cues*, their in-sentence *scopes* and the negated factual *events*. Most of the systems submitted for the shared task correspondingly implemented a pipeline consisting of three components, one for each subtask. One thing that set the system of Read et al. (2012) apart from other shared task submissions is that it included a *fourth* component; a dedicated classifier for identifying the *factuality* of a given context. It is this latter problem which is the main focus of the current paper, along with its interactions with the task of identifying events.

The field has witnessed a growing body of work dealing with uncertainty and speculative language over the recent years, and in particular so within the domain of biomedical literature. These efforts have been propelled not least by the several shared tasks that have targeted such phenomena. The shared task at the 2010 Conference on Natural Language Learning (CoNLL) focused on speculation detection for the domain of biomedical research literature (Farkas et al., 2010), with data sets based on the BioScope corpus (Vincze et al., 2008) which annotates so-called speculation *cues* along with their *scopes*. The BioNLP shared tasks of 2009 and 2011 mainly concerned recognizing bio-molecular events in text, but optional subtasks involved detecting whether these events were affected by speculation or negation. The data set used for this task is the Genia event corpus (Kim et al., 2008) which annotates the uncertainty of events according to the three labels *certain*, *probable* and *doubtful* (but without explicitly annotating cue words or scope as in BioScope).

The best performer in the BioNLP 2011 supporting task of detecting speculation modification of events, the system of Kilicoglu and Bergler (2011), achieved an end-to-end F_1 of 27.25 using a manually compiled dictionary of trigger expressions together with a set of rules operating on syntactic dependencies for identifying events and event modification. Turning to the task of identifying speculation cues in the BioScope data, current state-of-the-art systems, implementing simple supervised classification approaches on the token- or sequence-level, achieves F_1-scores of well above 80 (Tang et al., 2010; Velldal et al., 2012). For the task of resolving the scopes of these cues, the current best systems obtain end-to-end F_1-scores close to 60 in held-out testing (Morante et al., 2010; Velldal et al., 2012).

Note that the latter reference is from a forthcoming issue of Computational Linguistics specifically on modality and negation (Morante and Sporleder, 2012). In that same issue, Saurí and Pustejovsky (2012) present a linguistically motivated system for factuality profiling with manually crafted rules operating on dependency graphs. Conceptually treating factuality as a perspective that a particular source (speaker) holds toward an event, the system aims to make this attribution explicit. It is developed on the basis of the FactBank corpus (Saurí and Pustejovsky, 2009), containing manual annotations of pairs of events and sources along the dimensions of polarity (*positive*, *negative*, or *underspecified*) and certainty (*certain*, *probable*, *possible*, or *underspecified*.

Prabhakaran et al. (2010) report experiments with *belief tagging*, which in many ways is similar to factuality detection. Their starting point is a corpus of 10.000 words comprising a variety of genres (newswire text, emails, instructions, etc.) annotated for speaker belief of stated propositions (Diab et al., 2009): Propositional heads are tagged as *committed belief* (CB), *non-committed belief* (NCB), or *not applicable* (NA), meaning no belief is expressed by the speaker. To some degree, CB and NCB can be seen as similar to our categories of factuality and non-factuality, respectively. Applying a one-versus-all SVM classifier by 4-fold cross validation, and using wide range of both lexical and syntactical features, Prabhakaran et al. (2010) report F_1-scores of 69.6 for CB, 34.1 for NCB, and 64.5 for NA.

3 Data Sets and the Notion of Factuality

The data we will be using in the current study is taken from a recently released corpus of Conan Doyle (CD) stories annotated for negation (Morante and Daelemans, 2012). The data is annotated with *negation cues*, the in-sentence *scope* of those cues, as well as the negated *event*, if any. The cue is the word(s) or affix indicating a negation, The scope then indicates the maximal extent of that negation, while the event indicates the most basic negated element. In the annotation guidelines, Morante et al. (2011, p. 4) use the term *event* in a rather general sense; "[i]t can be a process, an action, or a state." The guidelines occasionally also refer to the notion of *negated elements* as encompassing "the main event or property actually negated by the negation cue" (Morante et al., 2011, p. 27). In the remainder of this paper we will simply take *event* to conflate all these senses.

Some examples of annotated sentences are shown below. Throughout the paper we will use angle brackets for marking negation cues, curly brackets for scopes, and underlines for events.

(1) {There was} ⟨no⟩ {answer}.

(2) {I do} ⟨n't⟩ {think that I am a coward} , Watson , but that sound seemed to freeze my very blood .

In the terminology of Saurí and Pustejovsky (2012), the negation cues are negative polarity particles, and all annotated events in the Conan Doyle data will have a negative polarity and thereby represent *counterfacts*, i.e., events with negative factuality. This should not be confused with non-factuality; a counterfactual statement is not uncertain.

Importantly, however, the Conan Doyle negation corpus does not explicitly contain any annotation of factuality. The annotation guidelines specify that "we focus only on annotating information relative to the negative polarity of an event" (Morante et al., 2011, p. 4). However, the guidelines also specify that events should only be annotated for negations that (i) have a scope and that (ii) occur in *factual statements* (Morante et al., 2011, p. 27). (As we only have annotations for the sentence-level it is possible to have a cue without a scope in cases where the cue negates a proposition in a preceding sentence.) The notion of (non-)factuality assumed in the current work will reflect the way it is defined in the Conan Doyle annotation guidelines. Morante et al. (2011) lists the following types of constructions as *not* expressing factual statements (we here show examples from CD^{DEV} for each case):

- Imperatives:

(3) {Do} ⟨n't⟩ {move} , I beg you , Watson .

- Non-factual interrogatives:

(4) {You do} ⟨n't⟩ {believe it} , do you , Watson ?

- Conditional constructions:

(5) If {the law can do} ⟨nothing⟩ we must take the risk ourselves .

- Modal constructions:

(6) {The fault from what I hear may} ⟨not⟩ {have been entirely on one side} .

- Wishes or desires:

(7) " I hope , " said Dr. Mortimer , " that {you do} ⟨not⟩ {look with suspicious eyes upon everyone [...]}

- Suppositions or presumptions:

(8) I think , Watson , {a brandy and soda would do him} ⟨no⟩ {harm} .

- Future tense:

(9) {The shadow} has departed and {will} ⟨not⟩ {return} .

Our goal then, will be to correctly identify these cases in order to separate between factual and non-factual contexts before identifying events. Note that, while an event, if present, must always be embedded in the scope, the indicators of factuality are typically found well outside of this scope. The examples also show that non-factuality here encompasses a wider range of phenomena than what is traditionally covered in work on identifying hedging or speculation.

The examples above illustrate how we can take the data to *implicitly* annotate factuality and non-factuality, and we here show how to take advantage of this to train a factuality classifier. For the experiments in this paper we will let positive examples correspond to negations that are annotated with both a scope and an event, while negative examples correspond to scoped negations with no event. For our training and development data (CD^{DEV}; more details below), this strategy gives 738 positive examples and 317 negatives, spread over 930 sentences.

Our weakly labeled data as defined above comes with several limitations of course. The implicit labeling of factuality will be limited to sentences that are negated. We will also not have access to an event in the cases of non-factuality. Neither, do we have any explicit annotation of factuality cue words for these examples. All we have are instances of negation that we know to be within some non-delimited factual or non-factual context. For our experiments here will therefore use the negation cue itself as a place-holder for the abstract notion of context that we are really trying to make predictions about.

Table 1 presents some basic statistics for the relevant data sets. For training and development we will use the negation annotated version of *The Hound of the Baskerville's* (CDH) and *Wisteria Lodge* (CDW) (Morante and Daelemans, 2012). We refer to the combination of these two data sets as CD^{DEV}. For held-out testing we will use the evaluation data sets prepared for the *SEM 2012 shared task; *The Cardboard Box* (CDC) and *The Red Circle* (CDR) (Morante and Blanco, 2012). We will use CD^{EVAL} to refer to the combination of CDC and CDR. Note

			Scoped Negations	
Data set	**Sentences**	**Negations**	**Factual**	**Non-factual**
CDH	3644	984	616	271
CDW	787	173	122	46
CD^{DEV}	4431	1157	738	317
CDC	496	133	87	41
CDR	593	131	86	35
CD^{EVAL}	1089	264	173	76

Table 1: Summary of the Conan Doyle negation data. Note that the total number of negations (column 3) can be smaller than the number of scoped negations (columns 4+5). The reason is that it is possible to have a cue without a scope in cases where the cue negates a proposition in a preceding sentence (which would not be reflected in these sentence-level annotations). The numbers in the column 'Factual' correspond to scoped negations that include an annotated event.

that the column *Factual* correspond to negations with both a scope and event (i.e., positive examples, in terms of factuality classification), while the *Non-factual* column correspond to negations with scope only and no event (negative examples).

4 Factuality Detection

Having described how we abstractly define our training data above, we can now move on to describe our experiments with training a factuality classifier. It is implemented as a linear binary SVM classifier, estimated using the SVM^{light} toolkit (Joachims, 1999). We start by describing the feature types in Section 4.1 and then present results in Section 4.2.

4.1 Features

The feature types we use are mostly variations over bag-of-words (BoW) features. We include left/right oriented BoW features centered on the negation cue, recording forms, lemmas, and PoS, and using both unigrams and bigrams. These features are extracted both from the sentence as a whole, and from a local window of six tokens to each side of the cue. The optimal window size and the order of n-grams was determined empirically.

The reason for including both local and sentence-level BoW features is that we would like to be able to assign different factuality labels to different instances of negation within the same sentence, but at the same time experiments showed sentence-level features to be very important.

Note that, ideally our features should be centered on the negated event, but since this information is only available for factual contexts, we instead take the negation cue as our starting point. In practice, this seems to provide a good approximation, however, given that the negated event is typically found in close vicinity of the negation cue.

In addition to the BoW type features we have features explicitly recording the first full-stop punctuation following the negation cue (i.e., '.', '!', or '?') as well as whether there is an *if* to the left. Note that, although this information is already implicit in the BoW features, the model appeared to benefit from having them explicitly coupled with the cue itself.

We also experimented with several other features that were not included in the final configuration. These included distance to co-occurring verbs, and modal verbs in particular. We also recorded the presence of speculative verbs based on various word lists manually extracted from the training data. None of these features appeared to contribute information not already present in the simple BoW features.

4.2 Results

Table 2 provides results for our factuality classifier using gold cues and gold scopes. In addition, we also include results for a baseline approach that simply considers all cases to be factual, i.e., the majority class. Note that, in this case the precision (of factuality labeling) is identical to the accuracy, which is close to 70% on both the development and held-out set. The recall for the majority-class baseline is of course at 100%, and the corresponding F_1 is approximately 82 on both data sets. In comparison, our classifier achieves an F_1 of 89.92 for the 10-fold cross-validation runs on the development data and 87.10 on the held-out test data. The accuracy is 83.98 and 80.72, respectively. Across both data sets it is clear that the classifier offers substantial improvements over the baseline. We do however, observe a drop in performance particularly with respect to precision when moving to the held-out set.When inspecting the scores for the two individual sections of the held-out set, CDC and CDR, we find that

Data set	Model	Prec	Rec	F_1	Acc
CD^{DEV}	Baseline	69.95	100.00	82.32	69.95
	Classifier	84.51	96.07	89.92	83.98
CD^{EVAL}	Baseline	69.48	100.00	81.99	69.48
	Classifier	80.60	94.74	87.10	80.72

Table 2: Results for factuality detection (using gold negation cues and scopes), reporting 10-fold cross-validation on CD^{DEV} and held-out testing on CD^{EVAL}.

Data set	Prec	Rec	F_1
CD^{DEV}	77.21	66.25	71.31
CD^{EVAL}	81.25	50.00	61.91

Table 3: Results for non-factuality detection (using gold negation cues and scopes). The scores are based on the same classifier predictions as in Table 2, but treats non-factuality as the positive class.

the classifier seems to have more difficulties with the former. Although recall is roughly the same across the two sections (94.25 and 95.24, respectively, which is again fairly close to the 10-fold recall of 96.07), precision suffers a much larger drop on CDC than CDR (78.85 versus 82.47). On the other hand, it is difficult to reliably assess performance on the individual test sets, given the limited amount of data: There are only 128 relevant test cases in CDC and 121 in CDR. However, there also seems to be signs of overfitting, in that an unhealthy number of the training examples end up as support vectors in the final model (close to 70%).

Note that the F_1-scores cited above targets *factuality* as the positive class label. However, given that this is in fact the majority class it might also be instructive to look at F_1-scores targeting *non-factuality*. (In other words, we will use exactly the same classifier predictions, but compute our scores by letting true positives correspond to former true negatives, false positives to former false negatives, and so on, thereby treating non-factuality as the positive class we are trying to predict.) Of course, while all accuracy scores will remain unchanged, the majority-class baseline yields an F_1 of 0 in this case, as there will be no true positives. Table 3 lists the non-factuality scores for the classifier.

Given that we are not aware of any other studies on (non-)factuality detection on this data we are not yet able to directly compare our results against those of other approaches. Nonetheless, we believe the state-of-the-art results cited in Section 2 for related tasks such as belief tagging and identifying speculation cues give reasons for being optimistic about the results obtained with the simple classifier used in these initial pilot experiments.

4.3 Error Analysis and Sample Size Effects

In order to gauge the effect that the size of the training set has on performance we also experimented with leaving out portions of the training examples in our 10-fold cross-validation runs. Figure 1 plots a learning curve showing how classifier performance on CD^{DEV} changes as we incrementally include more training examples. In order to more clearly bring out the contrasts in performance we here plot results against *non*-factuality scores. We also show the size of the training set on a logarithmic scale to better see whether improvements are constant for n-fold increases of data. As can be seen, the learning curve appears to be growing linearly with the increments in larger training samples and it seems safe to assume that the classifier would greatly benefit from

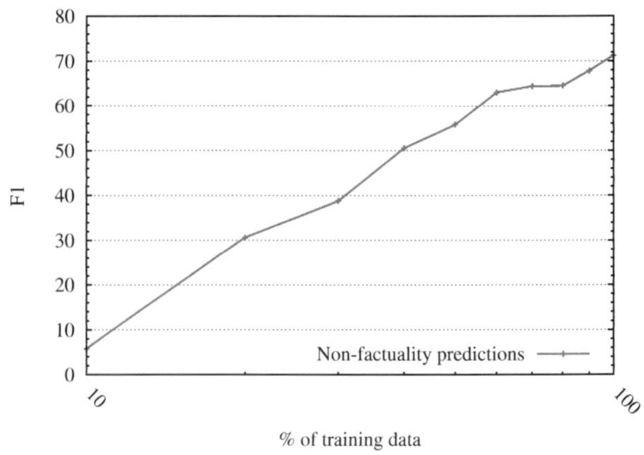

Figure 1: Learning curve showing the effect on F_1 for non-factuality labeling when withdrawing portions of the training partitions (shown on a logarithmic scale) across the 10-fold cross-validation cycles.

additional training data.

This impression is strengthened by a manual inspection of the misclassifications for CD^{DEV}. Quite a number of errors seem related to a combination of scarcity and noise in the data. As a fairly typical example, consider the following negation which the system incorrectly classifies as factual:

(10) " I presume , sir , " said he at last , " that {it was} ⟨not⟩ {merely for the purpose of examining my skull that you have done me the honour to call here last night and again today} ? "

One could have hoped that the BoW features recording the presence of *presume* would have tipped this prediction toward non-factual. However, while there are ten occurrences of *presume* in CD^{DEV}, only three of these are in contexts that we can actually use as part of our factuality training data. Apart from the one in Example (10), these are shown in (11) and (12) below, both of which indicate factual contexts (given the labeling of an event). We would at least consider Example (11) to reveal an error in the gold annotation here, however.

(11) " {There is} ⟨no⟩ {other claimant} , I presume ? "

(12) " {I presume} ⟨nothing⟩ .

We also get a few errors for incorrectly labeling a context as factual in cases where there are no obvious indicators of non-factuality but the annotation does not mark an event, as in:

(13) " ⟨Nothing⟩ {of much importance} , Mr. Holmes .

For some of the other errors we observed it would seem that introducing additional features that are sensitive to the syntactic structure could be beneficial. For example, consider sentence (14) below where we incorrectly classify the first negation as non-factual;

(14) [. . .] {I had brought it} only to defend myself if attacked and ⟨not⟩ {to shoot {an} ⟨un⟩{armed man} who was} running {away} .

The error is most likely due to overgeneralizing from the presence of *if*. By letting the lexical features be extracted from a context constrained by the syntax tree rather than a simple sliding window, such errors might be avoided.

For some more optimistic examples, note that the previously listed examples of non-factuality in (3) through (9) were all selected among cases that were correctly predicted by our classifier.

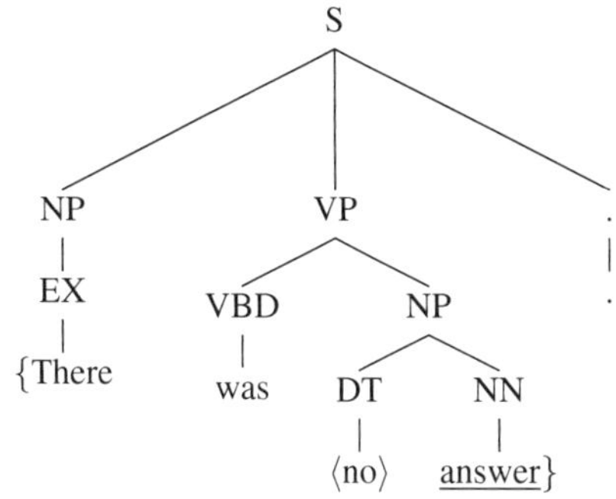

Figure 2: Example of parse tree in the negation data set.

In the next section we move on to describe a system for identifying negated events and assess the impact of the factuality classifier on this task (recall from Section 3 that only negations occurring in factual statements should be assigned an event).

5 Event Detection

To identify events in factual instances of negation[2] we employ an automatically-learned discriminative ranking function. As training data we select all negation scopes that have a single-token[3] event, and generate candidates from each token in the scope. The candidate that matches the event is labeled as correct; all others are labeled as incorrect. For the example sentence in Figure 2 there are three words in the scope and thus three candidates for events: *There*, *was* and *answer*.

5.1 Features

Candidates are primarily described in terms of paths in constituent trees.[4] In particular, we record the full path from a candidate token to the constituent whose projection matches the negation scope (i.e., the most-specific constituent that subsumes all can-

[2]Note that, although one could of course argue that negated events should also be identified for non-factual contexts, that is not how the task is construed in *SEM 2012 shared task or in the Conan Doyle data sets.

[3]To simplify the system we assume that all events are single tokens. It should be noted, however, that 9.85% of events in CD^{DEV} are actually composed of multiple tokens.

[4]Constituent trees from Charniak and Johnson's Max-Ent reranking parser (2005) were provided by the task organizers.

didates). In Figure 2 this is the S root of the tree; the path that describes the correct candidate is answer/NN/NP/VP/S. We also record delexicalized paths (e.g., ./NN/NP/VP/S) and generalized paths (e.g., ./NN//S), as well as bigrams formed of nodes on the path. Furthermore, we record some surface properties of candidates, namely; lemma, part-of-speech, direction and distance from cue, and position in scope. Finally, we record the lemma and part-of-speech of the token immediately preceding the candidate (development testing showed that information about the token following the candidate was not beneficial).

Based on the features above we learn an SVM-based scoring function using the implementation of ordinal ranking in SVM^{light} (Joachims, 2002). We use a linear kernel and empirically tune the regularization parameter C (governing the trade-off between margin size and errors).

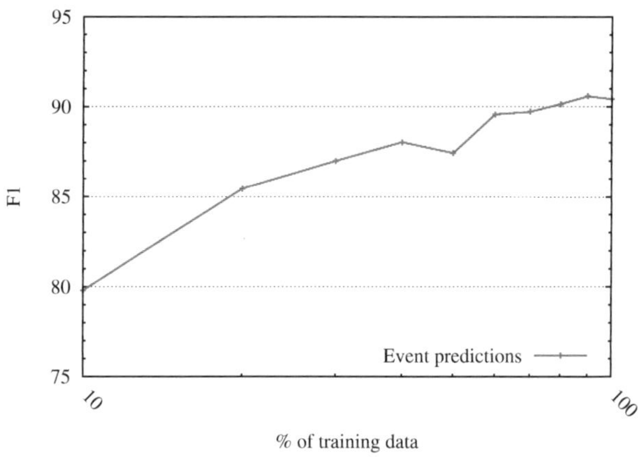

Figure 3: Learning curve showing the effect on F_1 for event detection when using gold factuality and withdrawing portions of the training partitions (shown on a logarithmic scale) across the 10-fold cross-validation cycles.

5.2 Results

Similarly to the learning curve shown above for factuality detection, Figure 3 plots the F_1 of event detection on CD^{DEV} when providing increasing amounts of training data and using gold standard information on factuality. (Note that, except for end-to-end results below, all scores reported in this paper assumes gold negation cues and gold scopes, given that we want to isolate the performance of the event ranker and/or factuality classifier.) We see that the performance is remarkably strong even at 10% of the total data, and increases steadily until around 60%, at which point it appears to be leveling off. It is unclear as to whether or not the ranker would benefit from additional data. We also note differences with respect to the factuality learning curve in Figure 1, both in terms of "entry performance" and overall trend. To some degree, there are general reasons as to why one could expect to see differences in learning curves for a discriminative ranking/regression set-up and a classifier set-up (assuming that the class distribution for the latter is unbalanced, as is typically the case). For a ranker, every item provides useful training data, in the sense that each item provides both positive and negative examples (in our case selected from the candidate tokens within a negation scope). For a classifier, the few items providing examples of the minority class will typically be the most valuable and it will therefore easily be more sensitive to having the training sample restrained. Even so, it seems clear that the factuality detection component and event detection component belong to different ends of the spectrum in terms of sensitivity to sample size.

Table 4 details the results of using the final ranking model to predict negated events. For a comparative baseline, we implemented a basic ranker that uses only the candidate lemma as a single feature. This baseline achieves an F_1 of 73.90 (P=74.01, R=73.80) on CD^{DEV} when using factuality information inferred from the gold-standard (and testing by 10-fold cross-validation). For comparison, the full ranking model achieves an F_1 of 90.42 (P=90.75, R=90.10) on the same data set, as seen in Table 4.

Of course, the results for event detection using gold-standard factuality also provides the upper bound for what we can achieve using system predicted factuality, i.e., applying the classifier described in Section 4. In order to assess the impact of the factuality classifier we also include results for event detection using the majority-class baseline, which means simply assuming that all instances of negations are factual. Table 4 lists results for event detection using system predicted factuality, compared to results using baseline and gold-standard factuality. We find that the factuality classifier greatly improves precision of the event de-

Data set	Factuality	Prec	Rec	F_1
CD^{DEV}	Baseline	62.24	90.10	73.62
	Classifier (10-fold)	78.48	82.98	80.67
	Gold	90.75	90.10	90.42
CD^{EVAL}	Baseline	58.26	84.94	69.11
	Classifier (Held-out)	68.72	80.24	74.03
	Gold	84.94	84.94	84.94

Table 4: Results for event detection using various methods for factuality detection.

tection. As can be expected, however, this comes with a cost in terms of recall. In both 10-fold cross-validation on CD^{DEV} and held-out testing on CD^{EVAL} we find large improvements in F_1, corresponding to error reductions of 26.73% and 15.93% respectively. As expected given the results discussed in Section 4, the improvement is slightly less pronounced for the held-out test results than the 10-fold cross-validated development results. Although the factuality classifier improves substantially over the baseline, it is also clear that a large gap remains toward the "upper bound" results of using gold-standard factuality. We take the results of the pilot experiments described in this paper as a proof-of-concept for using the CD data for training a factuality classifier, and at the same time have high expectations that future experimentation with additional (syntactically oriented) feature types should be able to further advance performance considerably.

Building on the system presented in Velldal et al. (2012), the initial *SEM 2012 shared task submission of Read et al. (2012) also included an SVM negation cue classifier (including support for morphological cues) along with an SVM-based ranking model over syntactic constituents for scope resolution. Coupled with the components for factuality and event detection described above, the end-to-end result for this system on CD^{EVAL} for identifying negated events is F_1=67.02 (P=60.58, R=75.00), making it the top-ranked submission in the shared task.

6 Conclusions and Future Directions

This paper has demonstrated that a classifier for discriminating between factuality and non-factuality can be trained by taking advantage of implicit information on factuality found in the negation annotations of the Conan Doyle corpus (Morante and Daelemans, 2012). Even though the pilot experiments described in this paper use just simple lexical features, the factuality classifier provides substantial improvements over the majority-class baseline. We also present a system for detecting negated events by learning an SVM-based discriminative ranking function over candidate tokens within the negation scope. We show that the factuality classifier proves very useful for improving the precision of event detection. In order to isolate the performance of the event ranker and factuality classifier we have focused on results for gold negation cues and scopes in this paper, although end-to-end results for the full system presented by Read et al. (2012) are also included. The system obtained the best results for identifying negative factual events in the 2012 *SEM shared task.

It is worth noting that there is nothing inherently negation specific about our factuality detection approach *per se*, save for how the training data happens to be extracted in the current study. One reason for using the implicit factuality information in the Conan Doyle negation corpus is the advantage of getting in-domain data, and this also allowed us to stay within the confines of the closed track for the *SEM shared task. For future experiments, however, we would also like to test cross-domain portability by both training and testing the factuality classifier using other annotated data sets such as FactBank, and also add features that incorporate predictions from speculation cue classifiers trained on BioScope.

Acknowledgments

We want to thank Roser Morante and Eduardo Blanco for their effort in organizing the *SEM 2012 shared task and providing the annotations. We also want to thank our colleagues at the University of Oslo (UiO), in particular Lilja Øvrelid and Stephan Oepen who contributed to the shared task submission. Large-scale experimentation was facilitated by the TITAN HPC cluster at UiO. We also thank the anonymous reviewers for their valuable comments and suggestions.

References

Eugene Charniak and Mark Johnson. 2005. Coarse-to-fine n-best parsing and MaxEnt discriminative reranking. In *Proceedings of the Forty-Third Annual Meeting of the Association for Computational Linguistics*, Ann Arbor, MI.

Mona T. Diab, Lori S. Levin, Teruko Mitamura, Owen Rambow, Vinodkumar Prabhakaran, and Weiwei Guo. 2009. Committed belief annotation and tagging. In *Proceedings of the Third Linguistic Annotation Workshop (LAW 2009)*, pages 68–73, Singapore.

Richárd Farkas, Veronika Vincze, György Móra, János Csirik, and György Szarvas. 2010. The CoNLL-2010 Shared Task: Learning to detect hedges and their scope in natural language text. In *Proceedings of the 14th Conference on Natural Language Learning*, pages 1–12, Uppsala.

Thorsten Joachims. 1999. Making large-scale SVM learning practical. In Bernhard Schölkopf, Christopher J. C. Burges, and Alexander J. Smola, editors, *Advances in Kernel Methods: Support Vector Learning*, pages 41–56. MIT Press, Cambridge, MA.

Thorsten Joachims. 2002. Optimizing search engines using clickthrough data. In *Proceedings of the Eighth ACM International Conference on Knowledge Discovery and Data Mining*, Alberta.

Halil Kilicoglu and Sabine Bergler. 2011. Adapting a general semantic interpretation approach to biological event extraction. In *Proceedings of the BioNLP Shared Task 2011*, pages 173–182, Portland, OR.

Jin-Dong Kim, Tomoko Ohta, and Jun'ichi Tsujii. 2008. Corpus annotation for mining biomedical events from literature. *BMC Bioinformatics*, 9(10).

Roser Morante and Eduardo Blanco. 2012. *SEM 2012 shared task: Resolving the scope and focus of negation. In *Proceedings of the First Joint Conference on Lexical and Computational Semantics*, Montreal.

Roser Morante and Walter Daelemans. 2012. ConanDoyle-neg: Annotation of negation in Conan Doyle stories. In *Proceedings of the Eighth International Conference on Language Resources and Evaluation*, Istanbul.

Roser Morante and Caroline Sporleder. 2012. Modality and negation: An introduction to the special issue. *Computational Linguistics*, 38(2):1–38.

Roser Morante, Vincent Van Asch, and Walter Daelemans. 2010. Memory-based resolution of in-sentence scope of hedge cues. In *Proceedings of the 14th Conference on Natural Language Learning*, pages 40–47, Uppsala.

Roser Morante, Sarah Schrauwen, and Walter Daelemans. 2011. Annotation of negation cues and their scope: Guidelines v1.0. Technical report, University of Antwerp. CLIPS: Computational Linguistics & Psycholinguistics technical report series.

Vinodkumar Prabhakaran, Owen Rambow, and Mona T. Diab. 2010. Automatic committed belief tagging. In *Proceedings of the 23rd International Conference on Computational Linguistics*, pages 1014–1022, Beijing.

Jonathon Read, Erik Velldal, Lilja Øvrelid, and Stephan Oepen. 2012. UiO_1: Constituent-based discriminative ranking for negation resolution. In *Proceedings of the First Joint Conference on Lexical and Computational Semantics*, Montreal. Submission under review.

Roser Saurí and James Pustejovsky. 2009. Factbank: a corpus annotated with event factuality. *Language Resources and Evaluation*, 43(3):227–268.

Roser Saurí and James Pustejovsky. 2012. Are you sure that this happened? assessing the factuality degree of events in text. *Computational Linguistics*, 38(2).

Buzhou Tang, Xiaolong Wang, Xuan Wang, Bo Yuan, and Shixi Fan. 2010. A cascade method for detecting hedges and their scope in natural language text. In *Proceedings of the 14th Conference on Natural Language Learning*, pages 13–17, Uppsala.

Erik Velldal, Lilja Øvrelid, Jonathon Read, and Stephan Oepen. 2012. Speculation and negation: Rules, rankers and the role of syntax. *Computational Linguistics*, 38(2).

Veronika Vincze, György Szarvas, Richárd Farkas, György Móra, and János Csirik. 2008. The BioScope corpus: Biomedical texts annotated for uncertainty, negation and their scopes. *BMC Bioinformatics*, 9 (Suppl. 11).

Improving Speculative Language Detection using Linguistic Knowledge

Guillermo Moncecchi
Facultad de Ingeniería
Universidad de la República
Montevideo, Uruguay

Jean-Luc Minel
Laboratoire MoDyCo
Université Paris Ouest
Nanterre La Défense, France

Dina Wonsever
Facultad de Ingeniería
Universidad de la República
Montevideo, Uruguay

Abstract

In this paper we present an iterative methodology to improve classifier performance by incorporating linguistic knowledge, and propose a way to incorporate domain rules into the learning process. We applied the methodology to the tasks of hedge cue recognition and scope detection and obtained competitive results on a publicly available corpus.

1 Introduction

A common task in Natural Language Processing (NLP) is to extract or infer factual information from textual data. In the field of natural sciences this task turns out to be of particular importance, because science aims to discover or describe facts from the world around us. Extracting these facts from the huge and constantly growing body of research articles in areas such as, for example, molecular biology, becomes increasingly necessary, and has been the subject of intense research in the last decade (Ananiadou et al., 2006). The fields of information extraction and text mining have paid particular attention to this issue, seeking to automatically populate structured databases with data extracted or inferred from text. In both cases, the problem of speculative language detection is a challenging one, because it may correspond to a subjective attitude of the writer towards the truth value of certain facts, and that information should not be lost when the fact is extracted or inferred.

When researchers express facts and relations in their research articles, they often use speculative language to convey their attitude to the truth of what is said. *Hedging*, a term first introduced by Lakoff (1973) to describe 'words whose job is to make things fuzzier or less fuzzy' is 'the expression of tentativeness and possibility in language use' (Hyland, 1995), and is extensively used in scientific writing. Hyland (1996a) reports one hedge in every 50 words of a corpus of research articles; Light et al. (2004) mention that 11% of the sentences in MEDLINE contain speculative language. Vincze et al. (2008) report that 18% of the sentences in the scientific abstracts section of the Bioscope corpus correspond to speculations.

Early work on speculative language detection tried to classify a sentence either as speculative or non-speculative (see, for example, Medlock and Briscoe (2007)). This approach does not take into account the fact that hedging usually affects propositions or claims (Hyland, 1995) and that sentences often include more than one of them. When the Bioscope corpus (Vincze et al., 2008) was developed the notions of *hedge cue* (corresponding to what was previously called just 'hedges' in the literature) and scope (the propositions affected by the hedge cues) were introduced. In this context, speculative language recognition can be seen as a two-phase process: first, the existence of a hedge cue in a sentence is detected, and second, the scope of the induced hedge is determined. This approach was first used by Morante et al. (2008) and subsequently in many of the studies presented in the CoNLL-2010 Conference Shared Task (Farkas et al., 2010a), and is the one used in this paper.

For example, the sentence

(1) This finding $\{_{suggests}$ suggests that the BZLF1

promoter $\{_{may}$ may be regulated by the degree of squamous differentiation$\}_{may}\}_{suggests}$.

contains the word 'may' that acts as a hedge cue (i.e. attenuating the affirmation); this hedge only affects the propositions included in the subordinate clause that contains it.

Each of these phases can be modelled (albeit with some differences, described in the following sections) as a sequential classification task, using a similar approach to that commonly used for named entity recognition or semantic labelling: every word in the sentence is assigned a class, identifying spans of text (as, for example, scopes) with, for example, a special class for the first and last element of the span. Correctly learning these classes is the computational task to be solved.

In this paper we present a methodology and machine learning system implementing it that, based on previous work on speculation detection, studies how to improve recognition by analysing learning errors and incorporating advice from domain experts in order to solve the errors without hurting overall performance. The methodology proposes the use of domain knowledge rules that suggest a class for an instance, and shows how to incorporate them into the learning process. In our particular task domain knowledge is linguistic knowledge, as hedging and scopes issues are general linguistic devices. In this paper we are going both terms interchangeably.

The paper is organized as follows. In Section 2 we review previous theoretical work on speculative language and the main computational approaches to the task of detecting speculative sentences. Section 3 briefly describes the corpus used for training and evaluation. In Section 4 we present the specific computational task to which our methodology was applied. In Section 5 we present the learning methodology we propose to use, and describe the system we implemented, including lexical, syntactic and semantic attributes we experimented with. We present and discuss the results obtained in Section 6. Finally, in Section 7 we analyse the approach presented here and discuss its advantages and problems, suggesting future lines of research.

2 Related work

The grammatical phenomenon of *modality*, defined as 'a category of linguistic meaning having to do with the expression of possibility and necessity' (von Fintel, 2006) has been extensively studied in the linguistic literature. Modality can be expressed using different linguistic devices: in English, for example, modal auxiliaries (such as 'could' or 'must'), adverbs ('perhaps'), adjectives ('possible'), or other lexical verbs ('suggest','indicate'), are used to express the different ways of modality. Other languages express modality in different forms, for example using the subjunctive mood. Palmer (2001) considers modality as the grammaticalization of speakers' attitudes and opinions, and epistemic modality, in particular, applies to 'any modal system that indicates the degree of commitment by the speaker to what he says'.

Although hedging is a concept that is closely related to epistemic modality, they are different: modality is a grammatical category, whereas hedging is a pragmatic position (Morante and Sporleder, 2012). This phenomenon has been theoretically studied in different domains and particularly in scientific writing (Hyland, 1995; Hyland, 1996b; Hyland, 1996a).

From a computational point of view, speculative language detection is an emerging area of research, and it is only in the last five years that a relatively large body of work has been produced. In the remainder of this section, we survey the main approaches to hedge recognition, particularly in English and in research discourse.

Medlock and Briscoe (2007) applied a weakly supervised learning algorithm to classify sentences as speculative or non-speculative, using a corpus they built and made publicly available. Morante and Daelemans (2009) not only tried to detect hedge cues but also to identify their scope, using a metalearning approach based on three supervised learning methods. They achieved an F1 of 84.77 for hedge identification, and 78.54 for scope detection (using gold-standard hedge signals) in the Abstracts sections of the Bioscope corpus.

Task 2 of the CoNLL-2010 Conference Shared Task (Farkas et al., 2010b) proposed solving the problem of in-sentence hedge cue phrase identification and scope detection in two different domains (biological publications and Wikipedia articles), based on manually annotated corpora. The evaluation criterion was in terms of precision, recall and F-measure, accepting a scope as correctly classified if the hedge cue and scope boundaries were both correctly identified.

The best result on hedge cue identification (Tang et al., 2010) obtained an F-score of 81.3 using a supervised sequential learning algorithm to learn BIO classes from lexical and shallow parsing information, also including certain linguistic rules. For scope detection, Morante et al. (2010) obtained an F-score of 57.3, using also a sequence classification approach for detecting boundaries (tagged in `FOL` format, where the first token of the span is marked with an `F`, while the last one is marked with an `L`). The attributes used included lexical information, dependency parsing information, and some features based on the information in the parse tree.

The approximation of Velldal et al. (2010) for scope detection was somewhat different: they developed a set of handcrafted rules, based on dependency parsing and lexical features. With this approach, they achieved an F-score of 55.3, the third best for the task. Similarly, Kilicoglu and Bergler (2010) used a pure rule-based approach based on constituent parse trees in addition to syntactic dependency relations, and achieved the fourth best F-score for scope detection, and the highest precision of the whole task (62.5). In a recent paper, Velldal et al. (2012) reported a better F-score of 59.4 on the same corpus for scope detection using a hybrid approach that combined a set of rules on syntactic features and n-gram features of surface forms and lexical information and a machine learning system that selected subtrees in constituent structures.

3 Corpus

The system presented in this paper uses the Bioscope corpus (Vincze et al., 2008) as a learning source and for evaluation purposes. The Bioscope corpus is a freely available corpus of medical free texts, biological full papers and biological abstracts, annotated at a token level with negative and speculative keywords, and at sentence level with their linguistic scope.

	Clinical	Full	Abstract
#Documents	954	9	1273
#Sentences	6383	2670	11871
%Hedge Sentences	13.4	19.4	17.7
#Hedge cues	1189	714	2769

Table 1: Bioscope corpus statistics about hedging

Table 1, extracted from Vincze et al. (2008), gives some statistics related to hedge cues and sentences for the three sub corpora included in Bioscope.

For the present study, we usee only the Abstract sub corpus for training and evaluation. We randomly separated 20% of the corpus, leaving it for evaluation purposes. We further sub-divided the remaining training corpus, separating another 20% that was used as a held out corpus. All the models presented here were trained on the resulting training corpus and their performance evaluated on the held out corpus. The final results were computed on the previously unseen evaluation corpus.

4 Task description

From a computational point of view, both hedge cue identification and scope detection can be seen as a *sequence classification problem*: given a sentence, classify each token as part of a hedge cue (or scope) or not. In almost every classification problem, two main approaches can be taken (although many variations and combinations exist in the literature): build the classifier as a set of handcrafted rules, which, from certain attributes of the instances, decide which category it belongs to, or learn the classifier from previously annotated examples, in a supervised learning approach.

The rules approach is particularly suitable when domain experts are available to write the rules, and when features directly represent linguistic information (for example, POS-tags) or other types of domain information. It is usually a time-consuming task, but it probably grasps the subtleties of the linguistic phenomena studied better, making it possible to take them into account when building the classifier. The supervised learning approach needs tagged data; in recent years the availability of tagged text has grown, and this type of method has become the state-of-the-art solution for many NLP problems.

In our particular problem, we have both tagged data and expert knowledge (represented by the body of work on modality and hedging), so it seems reasonable to see how we can combine the two methods to achieve better classification performance.

4.1 Identifying hedge cues

The best results so far for this task used a token classification approach or sequential labelling techniques, as Farkas et al. (2010b) note. In both cases, every token in the sentence is assigned a class label indicating whether or not that word is acting as a hedge cue. To allow for multiple-token hedge cues, we identify the first token of the span with the class `B` and every other token in the span with `I`, keeping the `O` class for every token not included in the span, as the following example shows:

(2) The/`O` findings/`O` indicate/`B` that/`I` MNDA/`O` expression/`O` is/`O` . . . [401.8]

After token labelling, hedge cue identification can be seen as the problem of assigning the correct class to each token of an unlabelled sentence. Hedge cue identification is a *sequential classification* task: we want to assign classes to an entire ordered sequence of tokens and try to maximize the probability of assigning the correct classes to every token in the sequence, considering the sequence as a whole, not just as a set of isolated tokens.

4.2 Determining the scope of hedge cues

The second sub-task involves marking the part of the sentence affected by the previously identified hedge cue. Scopes are also spans of text (typically longer than multi-word hedge cues), so we could use the same reduction to a token classification task. Being longer, `FOL` classes are usually used for classification, identifying the first token of the scope as `F`, the last token as `L` and any other token in the sentence as `O`. Scope detection poses an additional problem: hedge cues cannot be nested, but scopes (as we have already seen) usually are. In example 1, the scope of 'may' is nested within the scope of 'suggests'. To overcome this, Morante and Daelemans (2009) propose to generate a different learning example for each cue in the sentence. In this setting, each example becomes a pair ⟨labelled sentence, hedge cue position⟩. So, for example 1, the scope learning instances would be:

(3) ⟨This/`O` finding/`O` suggests/`F` that/`O` the/`O` BZLF1/`O` promoter/`O` may/`O` be/`O` regulated/`O` by/`O` the/`O` degree/`O` of/`O` squamous/`O` differentiation/`L`./`O`, 3⟩

(4) ⟨This/`O` finding/`O` suggests/`O` that/`O` the/`F` BZLF1/`O` promoter/`O` may/`O` be/`O` regulated/`O` by/`O` the/`O` degree/`O` of/`O` squamous/`O` differentiation/`L`./`O`, 8⟩

Learning on these instances, and using a similar approach to the one used in the previous task, we should be able to identify scopes for previously unseen examples. Of course, the two tasks are not independent: the success of the second one depends on the success of the first. Accordingly, evaluation of the second task can be done using gold standard hedge cues or with the hedge cues learned in the first task.

5 Methodology and System Description

To approach both sequential learning tasks, we follow a learning methodology (depicted in Figure 1), that starts with an initial guess of attributes for supervised learning and a learning method, and tries to improve its performance by incorporating domain knowledge. We consider that expressing this knowledge through rules (instead of learning features) is a better way for a domain expert to suggest new useful information or to generalize certain relations between attributes and classification results when the learning method cannot achieve this because of insufficient training data. These rules, of course, have to be converted to attributes to incorporate them into the learning process. These attributes are what we call *knowledge rules* and their generation will be described in the Analysis section.

5.1 Preprocessing

Before learning, we propose to add every possible item of external information to the corpus so as to integrate different sources of knowledge (either the result of external analysis or in the form of semantic resources). After this step, all the information is consolidated into a single structure, facilitating subsequent analysis. In our case, we incorporate POS-tagging information, resulting from the application of the GENIA tagger (Tsuruoka et al., 2005), and deep syntax information obtained with the application of the Stanford Parser (Klein and Manning, 2003), leading to a syntax-oriented representation of the training data. For a detailed description of the enriching process, the reader is referred to Moncecchi et al. (2010).

5.2 Initial Classifier

The first step for improving performance is, of course, to select an initial set of learning features, and learn from training data to obtain the first classifier, in a traditional supervised learning scenario. The sequential classification method will depend on the addressed task. After learning, the classifier is applied on the held out corpus to evaluate its performance (usually in terms of Precision, Recall and F1-measure), yielding performance results and a list of errors for analysis. This information is the source for subsequent linguistic analysis. As such, it seems important to provide ways to easily analyse instance attributes and learning errors. For our tasks, we have developed visualization tools to inspect the tree representation of the corpus data, the learning attributes, and the original and predicted classes.

5.3 Analysis

From the classifier results on the held-out corpus, an analysis phase starts, which tries to incorporate linguistic knowledge to improve performance.

One typical form of introducing new information is through learning features: for example, we can add a new attribute indicating if the current instance (in our case, a sentence token) belongs to a list of common hedge cues.

However, linguistic or domain knowledge can also naturally be stated as rules that suggest the class or list of classes that should be assigned to instances, based on certain conditions on features, linguistic knowledge or data observation. For example, based on corpus annotation guidelines, a rule could state that the scope of a verb hedge cue should be the verb phrase that includes the cue, as in the expression

(5) This finding $\{_{suggests}$ suggests that the BZLF1 promoter may be regulated by the degree of squamous differentiation$\}_{suggests}$.

We assume that these rules take the form 'if a condition `C` holds then classify instance `X` with class `Y`'. In the previous example, assuming a `FOL` format for scope identification, the token 'suggest' should be assigned class `F` and the token 'differentiation' should be assigned class `L`, assigning class `O` to every other token in the sentence.

The general problem with these rules is that as we do not know in fact if they always apply, we do not want to directly modify the classification results, but to incorporate them as attributes for the learning task. To do this, we propose to use a similar approach to the one used by Rosá (2011), i.e. to incorporate these rules as a new attribute, valued with the class predictions of the rule, trying to 'help' the classifier to detect those cases where the rule should fire, without ignoring the remaining attributes. In the previous example, this attribute would be (when the rule condition holds) valued `F` or `L` if the token corresponds to the first or last word of the enclosing verb phrase, respectively. We have called these attributes *knowledge rules* to reflect the fact that they suggest a classification result based on domain knowledge.

This configuration allows us to incorporate heuristic rules without caring too much about their potential precision or recall ability: we expect the classification method to do this for us, detecting correlations between the rule result (and the rest of the attributes) and the predicted class.

There are some cases where we do actually want to overwrite classifier results: this is the case when we know the classifier has made an error, because the results are not well-formed. For example, we have included a rule that modifies the assigned classes when the classifier has not exactly found one `F` token and one `L` token, as we know for sure that something has gone wrong. In this case, we decided to assign the scope based on a series of postprocessing rules: for example, assign the scope of the enclosing clause in the syntax tree as hedge scope, in the case of verb hedge cues.

For sequential classification tasks, there is an additional issue: sometimes the knowledge rule indicates the beginning of the sequence, and its end can be determined using the remaining attributes. For example, suppose the classifier suggests the class

Hedge	PPOS	GPPOS	Lemma	PScope	GPScope	Scope
O	VP	S	This	O	O	O
O	VP	S	finding	O	O	O
O	VP	S	suggest	O	O	O
O	VP	S	that	O	O	O
O	VP	S	the	O	F	F
O	VP	S	BZLF1	O	O	O
O	VP	S	promoter	O	O	O
B	VP	S	may	F	O	O
O	VP	S	be	O	O	O
O	VP	S	regulate	O	O	O
O	VP	S	by	O	O	O
O	VP	S	the	O	O	O
O	VP	S	degree	O	O	O
O	VP	S	of	O	O	O
O	VP	S	squamous	O	O	O
O	VP	S	differentiation	L	L	O
O	VP	S	.	O	O	O

Table 2: Evaluation instance where the scope ending could not be identified

scope in the learning instance shown in table 2 (using as attributes the scopes of the parent and grandparent constituents for the hedge cue in the syntax tree). If we could associate the F class suggested by the classifier with the grand parent scope rule, we would not be concerned about the prediction for the last token, because we would knew it would always correspond to the last token of the grand parent clause. To achieve this, we modified the class we want to learn, introducing a new class, say X, instead of F, to indicate that, in those cases, the L token must not be learned, but calculated in the postprocessing step, in terms of other attributes' values (in this example, using the hedge cue grandparent constituent limits). This change also affects the classes of training data instances (in the example, every training instance where the scope coincides with the grand parent scope attribute will have its F-classified token class changed to X).

In the previous example, if the classifier assigns class X to the 'the' token, the postprocessing step will change the class assigned to the 'differentiation' token to L, no matter which class the classifier had predicted, changing also the X class to the original F, yielding a correctly identified scope.

After adding the new attributes and changing the relevant class values in the training set, the process starts over again. If performance on the held out corpus improves, these attributes are added to the best configuration so far, and used as the starting point for a new analysis. When no further improvement can be achieved, the process ends, yielding the best

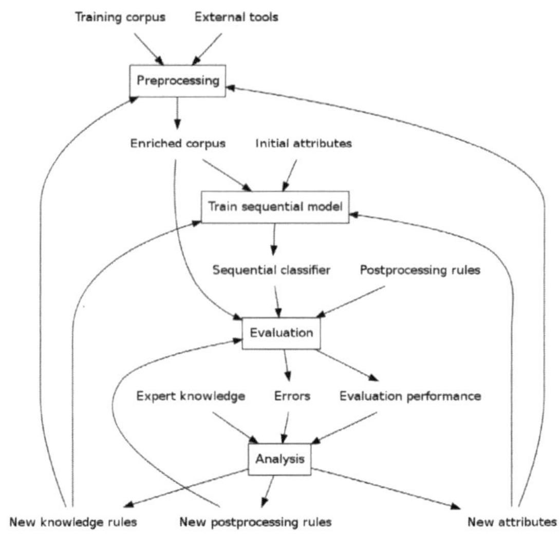

Figure 1: Methodology overview

classifier as a result.

We applied the proposed methodology to the tasks of hedge cue detection and scope resolution. We were mainly interested in evaluating whether systematically applying the methodology would indeed improve classifier performance. The following sections show how we tackled each task, and how we managed to incorporate expert knowledge and improve classification.

5.4 Hedge Cue Identification

To identify hedge cues we started with a sequential classifier based on Conditional Random Fields (Lafferty et al., 2001), the state-of-the-art classification method used for sequence supervised learning in many NLP tasks. The baseline configuration we started with included a size-2 window of surface forms to the left and right of the current token, pairs and triples of previous/current surface forms. This led to a highly precise classifier (an F-measure of 95.5 on the held out corpus). After a grid search on different configurations of surface forms, lemmas and POS tags, we found (somewhat surprisingly) that the best precision/recall tradeoff was obtained just using a window of size 2 of unigrams of surface forms, lemmas and tokens with a slightly worse precision than the baseline classifier, but compen-

Configuration	P	R	F1
Baseline	**95.5**	74.0	83.4
Conf1	94.7	80.3	86.9
Conf2	91.3	**84.0**	**87.5**

Table 3: Classification performance on the held out corpus for hedge cue detection. Conf1 corresponds to windows of Word, Lemma and POS attributes and Conf2 incorporates hedge cue candidates and cooccuring words

sated by an improvement of about six points in recall, achieving an F-score of 86.9.

In the analysis step of the methodology we found that most errors came from False Negatives, i.e. words incorrectly not marked as hedges. We also found that those words actually occurred in the training corpus as hedge cues, so we decided to add new rule attributes indicating membership to certain semantic classes. After checking the literature, we added three attributes:

- Hyland words membership: this feature was set to `Y` if the word was part of the list of words identified by Hyland (2005)
- Hedge cue candidates: this feature was set to `Y` if the word appeared as a hedge cue in the training corpus
- Words co-occurring with hedge cue candidates: this feature was set to `Y` if the word cooccured with a hedge cue candidate in the training corpus. This feature is based on the observation that 43% of the hedges in a corpus of scientific articles occur in the same sentence as at least another device (Hyland, 1995).

After adding these attributes and tuning the window sizes, performance improved to an F-score of 87.5 in the held-out corpus

5.5 Scope identification

To learn scope boundaries, we started with a similar configuration of a CRF classifier, using a window of size 2 of surface forms, lemmas and POS-tags, and the hedge cue identification attribute (either obtained from the training corpus when using gold standard hedge cues or learned in the previous step), achieving a performance of 63.7 in terms of F-measure. When we incorporated information in the form of a knowledge rule that suggested the scope of the constituent of the parsing tree headed by the parent node of the first word of the hedge cue, and an attribute containing the parent POS-tag, performance rapidly improved about two points measured in terms of F-score.

After several iterations, and analyzing classification errors, we included several knowledge rules, attributes and postprocessing rules that dramatically improved performance on the held-out corpus:

- We included attributes for the scope of the next three ancestors of the first word of the hedge cue in the parsing tree, and their respective POS-tags, in a similar way as with the parent. We also included a trigram with the ancestors POS from the word upward in the tree.
- For parent and grandparent scopes, we incorporated X and Y classes instead of F, and modified postprocessing to use the last token of the corresponding scope when one of these classes was learned.
- We modified the ancestors scopes to reflect some corpus annotation guidelines or other criteria induced after data examination. For example, we decided not to include adverbial phrases or prepositional phrases at the beginning of scopes, when they corresponded to a clause, as in

  (6) In addition,{unwanted and potentially hazardous specificities <u>may</u> be elicited...}

- We added postprocessing rules to cope with cases where (probably due to insufficient training data), the classifier missclasified certain instances. For example, we forced classification to use the next enclosing clause (instead of verb phrase), when the hedge cue was a verb conjugated in passive voice, as in

  (7) {GATA3 , a member of the GATA family that is abundantly expressed in the T-lymphocyte lineage , is <u>thought</u> to participate in ...}.

Configuration	Gold-P	P	R	F1
Baseline	66.4	68.6	59.6	63.8
Conf1	68.7	71.3	61.8	66.2
Conf2	73.3	75.6	65.4	70.1
Conf3	80.9	82.1	71.3	76.3
Conf4	**88.2**	**82.0**	**76.3**	**79.1**

Table 4: Classification performance on the held out corpus. The baseline used a window of Word, Lemma, POS attributes and hedge cue tag; Conf1 included parent scopes, Conf2 added grandparents information; Conf3 added postprocessing rules. Finally, Conf4 used adjusted scopes and incorporated new postprocessing rules

- We excluded references at the end of sentences from all the calculated scopes.

- We forced classification to the next `S`,`VP` or `NP` ancestor constituent in the syntax tree (depending on the hedge cue POS), when full scopes could not be determined by the statistical classifier (missing either `L` or `F`, or learning more than one of them in the same sentence).

Table 4 summarizes the results of scope identification in the held out corpus. The first results were obtained using gold-standard hedge cues, while the second ones used the hedge cues learned in the previous step (for hedge cue identification, we used the best configuration we found). In the gold-standard results, Precision, Recall and the F-measure are the same because every False Positive (incorrectly marked scope) implied a False Negative (the missed right scope).

6 Evaluation

To determine classifier performance, we evaluated the classifiers found after improvement on the evaluation corpus. We also evaluated the less efficient classifiers to see whether applying the iterative improvement had overfitted the classifier to the corpus. To evaluate scope detection, we used the best configuration found in the evaluation corpus for hedge cue identification. Tables 5 and 6 show the results for the hedge cue recognition and scope resolution, respectively. In both tasks, classifier performance

Configuration	P	R	F1
Baseline	**97.9**	78.0	86.8
Conf1	95.9	84.9	90.1
Conf2	94.1	**88.6**	**91.3**

Table 5: Classification performance on the evaluation corpus for hedge cue detection

Configuration	Gold-P	P	R	F1
Baseline	74.0	71.9	68.1	70.0
Conf1	76.5	74.4	70.2	72.3
Conf2	80.0	77.2	72.9	75.0
Conf3	83.1	80.0	75.2	77.3
Conf4	**84.7**	**80.1**	**75.8**	**77.9**

Table 6: Classification performance on the evaluation corpus for scope detection

improved in a similar way to the results obtained on the held out corpus.

Finally, to compare our results with state-of-the-art methods (even though that was not the main objective of the study), we used the corpus of de CoNLL 2010 Shared Task to train and evaluate our classifiers, using the best configurations found in the evaluation corpus, and obtained competitive results in both subtasks of Task 2. Our classifier for hedge cue detection achieved an F-measure of 79.9, better than the third position in the Shared Task for hedge identification. Scope detection results (using learned hedge cues) achieved an F-measure of 54.7, performing better than the fifth result in the corresponding task, and five points below the best results obtained so far in the corpus (Velldal et al.,

	Hedge cue identification	Scope detection
Best results	81.7/**81.0/81.3**	**59.6/55.2/57.3**
Our results	**83.2**/76.8/79.9	56.7/52.8/54.7

Table 7: Classification performance compared with best results in CoNLL Shared Task. Figures represent Precision/Recall/F1-measure

2012). Table 7 summarizes these results in terms of Precision/Recall/F1-measure.

7 Conclusions and Future Research

In this paper we have presented an iterative methodology to improve classifier performance by incorporating linguistic knowledge, and proposed a way to incorporate domain rules to the learning process. We applied the methodology to the task of hedge cue recognition and scope finding, improving performance by incorporating information of training corpus occurrences and co-occurrences for the first task, and syntax constituents information for the second. In both tasks, results were competitive with the best results obtained so far on a publicly available corpus. This methodology could be easily used for other sequential (or even traditional) classification tasks.

Two directions are planned for future research: first, to improve the classifier results by incorporating more knowledge rules such as those described by Velldal et al. (2012) or semantic resources, specially for the scope detection task. Second, to improve the methodology, for example by adding some way to select the most common errors in the held out corpus and write rules based on their examination.

References

S. Ananiadou, D. Kell, and J. Tsuj. 2006. Text mining and its potential applications in systems biology. *Trends in Biotechnology*, 24(12):571–579, December.

Richárd Farkas, Veronika Vincze, György Móra, János Csirik, and György Szarvas. 2010a. The CoNLL-2010 shared task: Learning to detect hedges and their scope in natural language text. In *Proceedings of the Fourteenth Conference on Computational Natural Language Learning*, pages 1–12, Uppsala, Sweden, July. Association for Computational Linguistics.

Richárd Farkas, Veronika Vincze, György Szarvas, György Móra, and János Csirik, editors. 2010b. *Proceedings of the Fourteenth Conference on Computational Natural Language Learning.* Association for Computational Linguistics, Uppsala, Sweden, July.

Ken Hyland. 1995. The author in the text: Hedging scientific writing. *Hongkong Papers in Linguistics and Language Teaching*, 18:33–42.

Ken Hyland. 1996a. Talking to the academy: Forms of hedging in science research articles. *Written Communication*, 13(2):251–281.

Ken Hyland. 1996b. Writing without conviction? Hedging in science research articles. *Applied Linguistics*, 17(4):433–454, December.

Ken Hyland. 2005. *Metadiscourse: Exploring Interaction in Writing.* Continuum Discourse. Continuum.

Halil Kilicoglu and Sabine Bergler. 2010. A high-precision approach to detecting hedges and their scopes. In *Proceedings of the Fourteenth Conference on Computational Natural Language Learning*, pages 70–77, Uppsala, Sweden, July. Association for Computational Linguistics.

Dan Klein and Christopher D. Manning. 2003. Accurate unlexicalized parsing. In *ACL '03: Proceedings of the 41st Annual Meeting on Association for Computational Linguistics*, pages 423–430, Morristown, NJ, USA. Association for Computational Linguistics.

John Lafferty, Andrew McCallum, and Fernando Pereira. 2001. Conditional random fields: Probabilistic models for segmenting and labeling sequence data. In *Proceedings of ICML-01*, pages 282–289.

George Lakoff. 1973. Hedges: A study in meaning criteria and the logic of fuzzy concepts. *Journal of Philosophical Logic*, 2(4):458–508, October.

Marc Light, Xin Y. Qiu, and Padmini Srinivasan. 2004. The language of bioscience: Facts, speculations, and statements in between. In Lynette Hirschman and James Pustejovsky, editors, *HLT-NAACL 2004 Workshop: BioLINK 2004, Linking Biological Literature, Ontologies and Databases*, pages 17–24, Boston, Massachusetts, USA, May. Association for Computational Linguistics.

Ben Medlock and Ted Briscoe. 2007. Weakly supervised learning for hedge classification in scientific literature. In *Proceedings of the 45th Annual Meeting of the Association of Computational Linguistics.*

Guillermo Moncecchi, Jean-Luc Minel, and Dina Wonsever. 2010. Enriching the bioscope corpus with lexical and syntactic information. In *Workshop in Natural Language Processing and Web-based Tecnhologies 2010*, pages 137–146, November.

Roser Morante and Walter Daelemans. 2009. Learning the scope of hedge cues in biomedical texts. In *Proceedings of the BioNLP 2009 Workshop*, pages 28–36, Boulder, Colorado, June. Association for Computational Linguistics.

Roser Morante and Caroline Sporleder. 2012. Modality and negation: An introduction to the special issue. *Computational Linguistics*, pages 1–72, February.

Roser Morante, Anthony Liekens, and Walter Daelemans. 2008. Learning the scope of negation in biomedical texts. In *EMNLP '08: Proceedings of the Conference on Empirical Methods in Natural Language Processing*, pages 715–724, Morristown, NJ, USA. Association for Computational Linguistics.

Roser Morante, Vincent Van Asch, and Walter Daelemans. 2010. Memory-based resolution of in-sentence scopes of hedge cues. In *Proceedings of the Fourteenth Conference on Computational Natural Language Learning*, pages 40–47, Uppsala, Sweden, July. Association for Computational Linguistics.

R. F. Palmer. 2001. *Mood and Modality*. Cambridge Textbooks in Linguistics. Cambridge University Press, New York.

Aiala Rosá. 2011. *Identificación de opiniones de diferentes fuentes en textos en español*. Ph.D. thesis, Universidad de la República (Uruguay), Université Paris Ouest (France), September.

Buzhou Tang, Xiaolong Wang, Xuan Wang, Bo Yuan, and Shixi Fan. 2010. A cascade method for detecting hedges and their scope in natural language text. In *Proceedings of the Fourteenth Conference on Computational Natural Language Learning*, pages 13–17, Uppsala, Sweden, July. Association for Computational Linguistics.

Yoshimasa Tsuruoka, Yuka Tateishi, Jin-Dong Kim, Tomoko Ohta, John McNaught, Sophia Ananiadou, and Jun'ichi Tsujii. 2005. Developing a robust Part-of-Speech tagger for biomedical text. In Panayiotis Bozanis and Elias N. Houstis, editors, *Advances in Informatics*, volume 3746, chapter 36, pages 382–392. Springer Berlin Heidelberg, Berlin, Heidelberg.

Erik Velldal, Lilja Øvrelid, and Stephan Oepen. 2010. Resolving speculation: Maxent cue classification and dependency-based scope rules. In *Proceedings of the Fourteenth Conference on Computational Natural Language Learning*, pages 48–55, Uppsala, Sweden, July. Association for Computational Linguistics.

Erik Velldal, Lilja Øvrelid, Jonathon Read, and Stephan Oepen. 2012. Speculation and negation: Rules, rankers, and the role of syntax. *Computational Linguistics*, pages 1–64, February.

Veronika Vincze, Gyorgy Szarvas, Richard Farkas, Gyorgy Mora, and Janos Csirik. 2008. The bioscope corpus: biomedical texts annotated for uncertainty, negation and their scopes. *BMC Bioinformatics*, 9(Suppl 11):S9+.

Kail von Fintel, 2006. *Modality and Language*. MacMillan Reference USA.

Bridging the Gap Between Scope-based and Event-based Negation/Speculation Annotations: A Bridge Not Too Far

Pontus Stenetorp[1] Sampo Pyysalo[2,3] Tomoko Ohta[2,3]
Sophia Ananiadou[2,3] and Jun'ichi Tsujii[2,3,4]
[1]Department of Computer Science, University of Tokyo, Tokyo, Japan
[2]School of Computer Science, University of Manchester, Manchester, United Kingdom
[3]National Centre for Text Mining, University of Manchester, Manchester, United Kingdom
[4]Microsoft Research Asia, Beijing, People's Republic of China
{pontus,smp,okap}@is.s.u-tokyo.ac.jp
sophia.ananiadou@manchester.ac.uk
jtsujii@microsoft.com

Abstract

We study two approaches to the marking of extra-propositional aspects of statements in text: the task-independent cue-and-scope representation considered in the CoNLL-2010 Shared Task, and the tagged-event representation applied in several recent event extraction tasks. Building on shared task resources and the analyses from state-of-the-art systems representing the two broad lines of research, we identify specific points of mismatch between the two perspectives and propose ways of addressing them. We demonstrate the feasibility of our approach by constructing a method that uses cue-and-scope analyses together with a small set of features motivated by data analysis to predict event negation and speculation. Evaluation on BioNLP Shared Task 2011 data indicates the method to outperform the negation/speculation components of state-of-the-art event extraction systems.
The system and resources introduced in this work are publicly available for research purposes at: *https://github.com/ninjin/eepura*

1 Introduction

Understanding extra-propositional aspects of texts is key to deeper understanding of statements contained in natural language texts. Extra-propositional aspects such as the polarity of key statements have long been acknowledged to be critical for user-facing applications such as information retrieval (Friedman et al., 1994; Hersh, 1996). In recognition of this need, a number of recent information extraction (IE) resources involving structured representations of text statements have explicitly included some marking of certainty and polarity (LDC, 2005; Kim et al., 2009; Saur and Pustejovsky, 2009; Kim et al., 2011a; Thompson et al., 2011).

Although extra-propositional aspects are recognised as important, there is no clear consensus on how to address their annotation and extraction from text. Some comparatively early efforts focused on the detection of negation *cue* phrases associated with specific (previously detected) terms through regular expression-based rules (Chapman et al., 2001). A number of later efforts identified the scope of negation cues with phrases in constituency analyses in sentence structure (Huang and Lowe, 2007). Drawing in part on this work, the BioScope corpus (Vincze et al., 2008) applied a representation where both cues and their associated *scopes* are marked as contiguous spans of text (Figure 1 bottom). This approach was also applied in the CoNLL-2010 Shared Task (Farkas et al., 2010), in which 13 participating groups proposed approaches for Task 2, which required the identification of uncertainty cues and their associated scopes in text. In the following, we will term this task-independent, linguistically-motivated approach as the *cue-and-scope* representation (please see Vincze et al. (2008) for details regarding the representation).

For IE efforts, more task-oriented representations are commonly applied. In an effort to formalise and drive research for extracting structured representations of statements regarding molecular biology, the ongoing series of BioNLP shared tasks have addressed biomedical Event Extraction (EE) (Kim et al., 2009; Kim et al., 2011a). The extra-propositional targets of negation and speculation

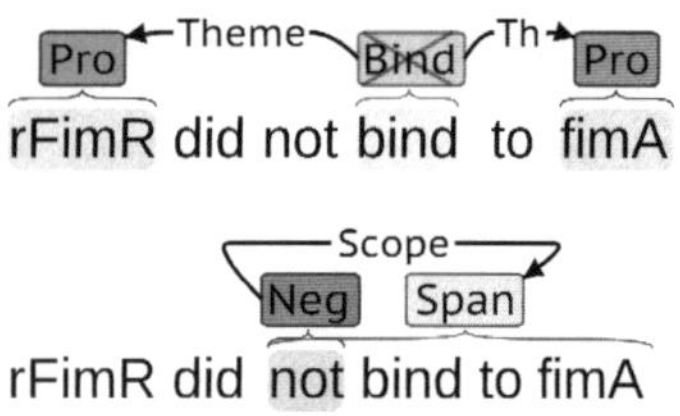

Figure 1: Example illustrating cue-and-scope and event-based negation marking. "Crossing-out" marks events as negated. PRO, TH and NEG are abbreviations for PROTEIN, THEME and NEGATION, respectively.

of extracted events were already included in the first task in the series, using a representation where events can be assigned "flags" to mark them as being negated, speculated, or both (Figure 1 upper). Due to space limitations we refer the reader to Kim et al. (2009) for a detailed explanation of the representation; similar representations have been applied also in previous event extraction tasks (LDC, 2005).

There are a number of ways in which task-oriented, event-based approaches could benefit from the existing linguistically-oriented cue-and-scope methods for identifying extra-propositional aspects of text statements. However, there has been surprisingly little work exploring the combination of the approaches, and comparatively few methods addressing the latter task in detail. Only three out of the 24 participants in the BioNLP Shared Task 2009 submitted results for the non-mandatory negation/speculation task, and although negation and speculation were also considered in three main tasks for the 2011 follow-up event (Kim et al., 2011a), the trend continued, with only two participants addressing the negation/speculation aspects of the task. We are aware of only two studies exploring the relationship between the cue-and-scope and event-based representations: in a manual analysis of scope overlap with tagged events, Vincze et al. (2011) identified a number of issues and mismatches in annotation scope and criteria, which may explain in part the lack of methods combining these two lines of research. Kilicoglu and Bergler (2010) approached the problem from the opposite direction and used an existing EE system to extract cue-and-scope annotations in the CoNLL-2010 Shared Task.

In this work, we take a high-level perspective, seeking to bridge the linguistically oriented framework and the more application-oriented event framework to overcome the mismatches demonstrated by Vincze et al. (2011). Specifically, we aim to determine how cue-and-scope recognition systems can be used to produce a state-of-the-art negation/speculation detection system for the EE task.

2 Resources

Several existing resources can support the investigation of the relationship between the linguistically-oriented and task-oriented perspectives on negation/speculation detection. In this study, we make use of the following resources.

First, we study the three BioNLP 2011 Shared Task corpora that include annotation for negation and speculation: the GE, EPI and ID main task corpora (Table 1). Second, we make use of supporting analyses provided for these corpora in response to a call sent by the BioNLP Shared Task organisers to the developers of third-party systems (Stenetorp et al., 2011). Specifically, we use the output of the BiographTA NeSp Scope Labeler (here referred to as *CLiPS-NESP*) (Morante and Daelemans, 2009; Morante et al., 2010) provided by the University of Antwerp CLiPS center. This system provides cue-and-scope analyses for negation and speculation and was demonstrated to have state-of-the-art performance at the relevant CoNLL-2010 Shared Task. Finally, we make use of the event analyses created by systems that participated in the BioNLP Shared Task, made available to the research community for the majority of the shared task submissions (Pyysalo et al., 2012). These analyses represent the state-of-the-art in event extraction and their capability to detect event structures as well as marking them for negation and speculation.

The above three resources present us with many opportunities to relate scope-based annotations to three highly relevant event-based corpora containing negation/speculation annotations.

3 Manual Analysis

To gain deeper insight into the data and the challenges in combining the cue-and-scope and event-oriented perspectives, we performed a manual analysis of the corpus annotations using the manually

Name	Negated Events		Speculated Events		Negated Spans	Speculated Spans	Publication
EPI	103	(5.6%)	70	(3.8%)	561	1,032	Ohta et al. (2011)
GE	759	(7.4%)	623	(6.0%)	1,308	1,968	Kim et al. (2011b)
ID	69	(3.3%)	26	(1.2%)	415	817	Pyysalo et al. (2011)

Table 1: Corpora used for our experiments along with annotation statistics for their respective training sets. The parenthesised values are the relative proportion of negated/speculated event annotations.

Occ. (Ratio)	EPI	ID
Covered	26 (15.03%)	52 (56.52%)
Not-covered	135 (78.03%)	38 (41.30%)
Error-in-gold	12 (6.94%)	2 (2.18%)
Morphological	48 (27.75%)	11 (11.96%)
Hypothesis	44 (25.43%)	15 (16.30%)
Ellipsis	5 (2.89%)	0 (0.00%)
Argument-only	2 (1.16%)	10 (10.87%)

Table 2: Results from the Manual Data Analysis of the EPI and ID test sets.

created BioNLP Shared Task training data event annotations, and the automatic annotations created for this data by the CLiPS-NESP system. The test data was held out and was not directly examined at any point of our study. We performed the analysis specifically on the EPI and ID corpora, as the GE corpus training set texts overlap with the training data for the CLiPS-NESP system (BioScope corpus), and results on this data would thus not reflect the performance of the system on unseen data, and a comparison of the GE and BioScope gold annotations was previously performed by Vincze et al. (2011).

The analysis was performed by an experienced annotator with a doctoral degree in a related field in biology, who individually examined each of the events marked as negated and speculated in the EPI and ID training corpora. For the analysis, the CLiPS-NESP system output was super-imposed onto the BioNLP Shared Task event annotations.

The annotator was asked to assign three primary flags for each event that was marked as negated or speculated: *Covered* if the event trigger was covered by span(s) of the correct type with a correct cue in the cue-and-span analysis, *Not-covered* if not *Covered*, and *Error-in-gold* if the negation/speculation flag on the event annotation was itself incorrect. We also identified a number of additional properties that initial analysis suggested to frequently characterise instances where the coverage of the cue-and-scope system is lacking: *Morphological* was assigned if the negation/speculation of an event could be inferred only from the morphology of the word expressing the event, rather than from cue words in its context (e.g. *unphosphorylated*, *non-glycosylated*); *Hypothesis* for cases where speculation is marked for events stated as hyphotheses[1] under consideration, e.g. "We analysed the methylation status of MGMT"; *Ellipsis* for cases where the modified expression is elided (e.g. "A was phosphorylated but B was not"); and *Argument-only* if the CLiPS-NESP output had marked the argument of an event as negated rather than the event trigger (we use argument in the sense it is used in the BioNLP Shared Tasks, for example, in Figure 1 upper, the two arguments of the event are "fMimR" and "fimA").

The results of the analysis are summarised in Table 2. We find that that the system shows a clear difference in coverage depending on the dataset. For the ID dataset, a majority of the annotations are covered by the appropriate spans, while only a small minority are covered for EPI. Instead, the EPI dataset contains a significant portion of events where extra-propositional aspects can only be distinguished by the morphology of the word expressing the event (all *Morphological* cases were negation) as well as events marked as speculated due to being expressed as hypotheses under study.

The analysis thus identified specific ways in which the applicability of negation-detection systems using a span-and-scope representation could be improved for some tasks.

[1]While it is arguable whether such cases represent speculation (Vincze et al., 2008), separation from affirmatively made claims is clearly motivated for many applications.

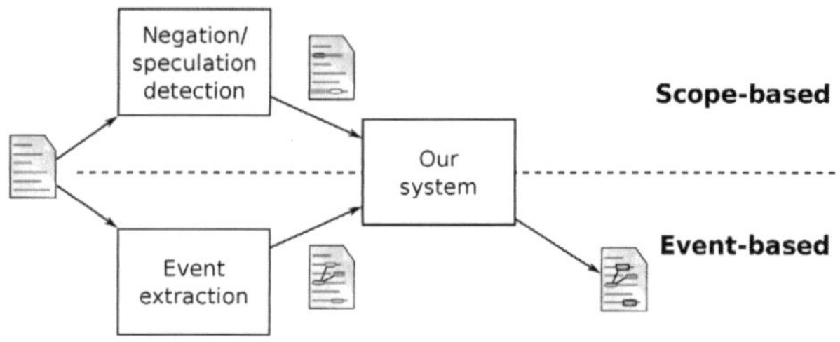

Figure 2: An illustration of our approach.

4 Methods

We next introduce the methods we apply for assigning negation and speculation flags to extracted events.

4.1 Approach

To focus on the extra-propositional aspects of event extraction, we only consider the assignment of the negation and speculation flags, not the extraction of the event structures that these mark. To our knowledge, no previous work studying this subtask in isolation from event extraction exists. Thus, in order to be able to relate the performance of the methods we consider to the performance of previously proposed approaches, it is necessary to base the negation and speculation detection on an event extraction analysis. For this reason, we construct our methods using system outputs for systems participating in the BioNLP Shared Task 2011, in effect creating a negation/speculation processing stage for a pipeline system where the previous stage is the completion of event analysis without negation/speculation detection (Figure 2).

Our methods thus take extracted events as input and attempt to enrich the output with negation and speculation annotations. This enables us to produce a general system with the potential to be applied together with any existing event extraction system. Additionally, this allows us to directly compare our system output with that of the negation/speculation components of previously proposed monolithic systems by removing the existing negation and speculation output from submissions including this and recreating these annotations using our methods.

4.2 Rule-based Methods

The most straightforward way of carrying over information from scope-based to event-based annotations is to consider any event structure for which the word or words stating the event (i.e. the event trigger) is within the scope of a negation or speculation be negated or speculated (respectively). We implemented this simple heuristic as our initial rule-based method.

One relatively common category of cases where this heuristic fails that was identified in analysis relates to events that take other events as arguments. Consider, for example, the case illustrated in Figure 3. The speculation span is correctly identified as covering the statement "FimR modulates mfa1 expression", and the event expressed through "modulates" is identified as speculated. However, the nested event, the expression of *mfa1*, is not speculated. To cover this case, we implemented what we refer to as the *root-heuristic*, which prevents the propagation of negation/speculation marking from scopes to events that are the arguments of another event contained in the same scope. The second rule-based method we consider incorporates this additional heuristic.

Preliminary development set experiments indicated that while the root-heuristic could improve precision, the performance of the rule-based methods remained poor, in particular on the EPI dataset. The results of the manual analysis (Section 3) suggested this to trace in particular to two main issues, namely differences between annotation criteria between BioScope and the shared task data (as noted also by Vincze et al. (2011)) and events which are negated not by external cues but by morphological alternations of the event trigger, such as "unphosphorylated" expressing the absence of phosphorylation. As it would have been difficult to systematically incorporate both morphology and context into the rule-based method without compromising the generality of the approach, we opted to move to a machine learning framework for further method development. This allows us to continue to make use of the existing cue-and-scope annotations while exploring the effects of other aspects of the text and maintaining generality through retraining.

4.3 Machine Learning-based Methods

In developing a machine learning-based approach to the negation/speculation task, we aimed to identify and evaluate a minimal set of features directly mo-

Feature	Example Value(s)
Heuristic	ROOT/NON-ROOT
Heuristic-Cue	possibility
Heuristic-Span	One, possibility, ...
Trigger-Text	non-phosphorylated
Trigger-Prefixes	no, non, non-, ...
Trigger-Preceding-Context	is, that, ...
Trigger-Proceeding-Context	mfa1, expression, ...

Table 3: Machine learning features. The features are categorised into three groups: features based on cue-and-scope based heuristics (top), non-contextual features derived from the event trigger (middle), and features derived from the context of the event trigger (bottom). These three feature sets are abbreviated as E, M and C, respectively.

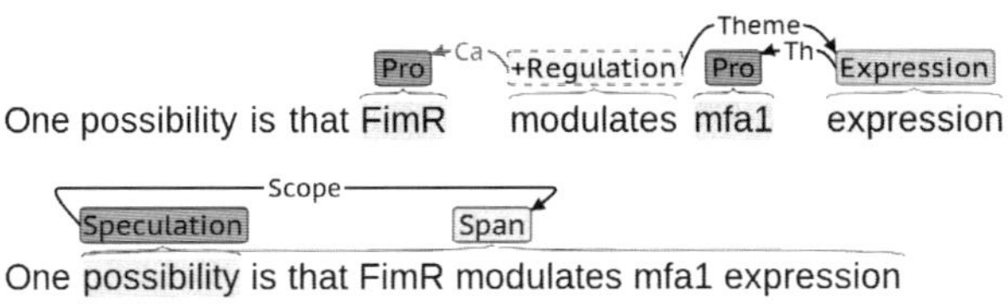

Figure 3: Example of a speculation span containing two events, of which only one is speculated (marked by a dashed border).

tivated by the analysis of the data and to use the cue-and-scope analyses as much as possible. In particular, we wanted to avoid features requiring computationally expensive analyses such as full parsing or replicating the type of analyses performed by the CLiPS-NESP system, focusing rather on specific points where its output does not meet the needs of the event-based approach.

We introduced features representing the heuristics described in Section 4.2, marking each case as being either a root or non-root event in its scope (if any). Drawing further on the cue-and-scope analysis, we included as features the cue word and bag-of-words features for all tokens in the scope (using simple white-space tokenisation). To address the issues identified in manual analysis, we introduced features for the event trigger text as well as character-based prefixes of lengths 2 to 7 of the, intended primarily to capture morphological negation.

All features presented above are derived only from those parts of the sentence already marked either by the event extraction or the cue-and-scope system. However, due to the differences in annotation guidelines for speculation annotations, we expect that the scope-based system will fail to mark a significant portion of the speculation annotations. To allow the system to learn to detect these, we introduce a minimal set of contextual features, limited to a bag-of-words representation of the three words preceding and following the event trigger.

5 Experiments

We perform two sets of experiments, the first to evaluate our approach on gold annotations to give a fair upper-limit to how well our negation/speculation detection system could perform under ideal settings, and the second to enrich the output of an event extraction system with negation and speculation annotations, to evaluate real-world performance and to allow direct comparison of our methods with those incorporated in monolithic event extraction and negation/speculation detection systems.

5.1 Corpora

For our experiments we used the GE, EPI and ID corpora of the BioNLP Shared Task 2011 (Table 1). We note that while the GE training set texts overlap with the BioScope corpus used to train the CLiPS-NESP system, the GE test set does not, and thus test set results are not expected to be overfit.

We noted when performing development set experiments that training machine learning-based methods on the negation/speculation annotations of the event-annotated corpora was problematic due to the sparseness of these flags in the annotation. To address this issue, we merge the training data of the three corpora in all experiments with machine learning methods.

5.2 Baseline methods

We use the event analyses created by the UTurku (Björne and Salakoski, 2011) and UConcordia (Kilicoglu and Bergler, 2011) systems for the BioNLP 2011, the only systems that included negation and speculation analyses. To investigate the impact on a system that did not include a negation/speculation component, we further consider analyses created

Negation (R/P/F)	EPI	GE	ID
H	29.23/31.67/30.40	53.92/52.84/53.38	44.00/31.88/36.97
HR	27.69/32.73/30.00	53.24/71.89/61.18	44.00/37.93/40.74
M	47.69/20.00/28.18	43.00/25.25/31.82	46.00/26.74/33.82
ME	**60.00**/66.10/62.90	58.36/70.08/63.69	54.00/69.23/60.67
MC	40.00/**74.29**/52.00	58.36/76.34/66.15	52.00/61.90/56.52
MCE	58.46/73.08/**64.96**	**61.77/83.03/70.84**	**58.00/70.73/63.74**

Table 4: Results for Negation for our two heuristics and the four combinations of machine learning features.

Speculation (R/P/F)	EPI	GE	ID
H	13.46/6.48/8.75	**33.77**/18.12/23.58	**54.17**/6.50/11.61
HR	11.54/5.66/7.59	32.79/29.45/31.03	**54.17**/7.98/13.90
M	1.92/0.62/0.93	25.65/10.84/15.24	45.83/10.58/17.19
ME	3.85/12.50/5.88	22.08/42.24/29.00	29.17/28.00/28.57
MC	**51.92/52.94/52.43**	27.27/50.30/35.37	37.50/31.03/33.96
MCE	48.08/51.02/49.50	31.82/**53.85/40.00**	33.33/**42.11/37.21**

Table 5: Results for Speculation for our two heuristics and the four combinations of ML features.

by the FAUST system, which achieved the highest performance at two of the three tasks considered (Riedel et al., 2011). The UTurku system is a pipeline ML-based EE system, while the UConcordia system is strictly rule-based. FAUST is an ML-based model combination system incorporating information from the parser-based Stanford system (McClosky et al., 2011) and the jointly-modelled UMass system (Riedel and McCallum, 2011).

We also performed preliminary experiments for the other released submissions to the BioNLP 2011 Shared Task, but due to space limitations focus only on the three above-mentioned systems.

5.3 Evaluation criteria

We use the primary evaluation criteria of the BioNLP 2011 Shared Task (Kim et al., 2011a) to assure comparability, reporting all results using the standard precision, recall and their harmonic mean (F-score).

5.4 Methods

We apply the rule-based simple heuristic method and its root extension (Section 4.2) as well as Support Vector Machines (SVM) trained with the features introduced in Section 4.3. For the SVM, we separately evaluate models based on all permutations of the feature sets introduced in Table 3. In the results tables we abbreviate the feature set names as done in Table 3 and use H for the heuristic method and R for its root extension. As our machine learning component we use LIBLINEAR (Fan et al., 2008) with a L2-regularised L2-loss SVM model. We optimise the SVM regularisation parameter C using 10-fold cross-validation on the training data.

We use the training, development and test set partition provided by the shared task organisers. In line with standard ML methodology the test set was held out during development and was only used when carrying out the final experiments prior to submitting the manuscript.

6 Results and Discussion

Our initial experiments, building on gold event data (Tables 4 and 5), support our manual analysis, showing nearly uniform performance improvement with additional features. First, we find that the root-heuristic gives an improvement over the original heuristic in four out of six cases. To justify our usage of the cue-and-scope based heuristic feature (E) we find that adding it as a feature improves on the M feature set and the MC feature set, showing that even given context, the cue-and-scope perspective is still useful. The only anomaly is for speculation on the EPI dataset, where adding this heuristic feature actually hampers performance, possibly relating to the

Negation (R/P/F)	EPI	GE	ID
UConcordia	16.92/61.11/26.51	18.43/**43.44**/25.88	22.00/23.91/22.92
UConcordia*	**20.00/70.59/31.17**	**20.14**/42.96/**27.42**	**28.00/31.58/29.68**
UTurku	12.31/38.10/18.60	**22.87/48.85/31.15**	**26.00/44.83/32.91**
UTurku*	**43.08/48.28/45.53**	21.16/38.56/27.33	**26.00**/41.94/32.10
FAUST*	29.23/59.38/39.18	21.50/41.18/28.25	**28.00/46.67/35.00**

Table 6: Results of the Negation enrichment experiment.

Speculation (R/P/F)	EPI	GE	ID
UConcordia	**5.77/8.33/6.82**	**21.10/38.46/27.25**	**8.33**/2.00/3.23
UConcordia*	1.92/4.55/2.70	12.99/29.20/17.98	**8.33/2.22/3.51**
UTurku	30.77/**48.48**/37.65	**17.86/32.54/23.06**	**12.50/18.75/15.00**
UTurku*	**46.15**/47.06/**46.60**	11.04/26.56/15.60	8.33/3.33/4.76
FAUST*	36.54/48.72/41.76	10.39/26.50/14.93	**12.50**/12.50/12.50

Table 7: Results of the Speculation enrichment experiment.

(R/P/F)	EPI	ID
UConcordia	**20.83**/42.14/27.88	49.00/40.27/44.21
UConcordia*	**20.83/42.94/28.05**	**49.20/41.78/45.19**
UTurku	52.69/**53.98**/53.33	**37.85/48.62/42.57**
UTurku*	**54.72**/53.86/**54.29**	37.79/47.76/42.19
FAUST	28.88/44.51/35.03	48.03/**65.97**/55.59
FAUST*	**31.64/45.17/37.21**	**49.20**/64.66/**55.88**

Table 8: Overall scores for the EPI and ID data sets.

F	EPI	GE	ID
UConcordia	57.43	60.68	67.28
UTurku	81.31	66.27	55.84
FAUST	74.91	66.14	67.13

Table 9: Estimated F-score upper-bound for an oracle system precision assigning negation/speculation annotations to events predicted by an up-stream EE system.

sparseness of useful annotations due to the differing annotation guidelines, as noted in manual analysis. The numbers from these initial experiments serve as an upper bound when we proceed to our enrichment experiments, as they do not suffer from the possibility of producing false positives negation/speculation annotations for false positive event structures.

In addition to the above in preliminary experiments we also considered two features inspired by findings made by Vincze et al. (2011). A distance-based feature, measuring the distance in tokens between the cue-word and the event trigger, and also trigger suffixes to capture some cases of morphological speculation ("induced" vs. "inducible"). However, we failed to establish any consistent benefits from these features and only for the EPI dataset did the suffix features improve performance.

For the enrichment evaluation, adding negation/speculation flags to the output of event extraction systems (Tables 6 and 7), our results are somewhat more modest. For negation we see an improvement in four out of six cases, and for speculation in two out of six. Despite the fact that a major limitation to our approach are the false positive events that are propagated from the original EE system, we manage to improve the global score for all data sets where a global score is provided by the organisers (Table 8). We improve a full point in F-score for UTurku on EPI, but only sub-percentage for Faust on ID, the latter most likely since ID contains fewer negation and speculation annotations and the global scores are microaverages over all annotations.

As a final analysis we estimate the upper-bound in F-score performance for all three EE systems (Table 9). We do so by assuming that the recall for events marked by negation and speculation is equal to that of the overall recall of the up-stream EE system and that negation/speculation annotations assigned by an oracle. What we can see is that there is still room for improvement, both for our enrichment approach and for the EE system's internal negation/speculation components, although recall of the EE output is a limiting factor we can expect further efforts towards improving the extra-propositional aspects of the system to yield performance improvements.

7 Conclusions and Future Work

In this study, we have considered two broad lines of research on extra-propositional aspects of key statements in text, one using the task-independent, linguistically-motivated cue-and-scope representation applied in the recent CoNLL-2010 Shared Task, and the other using the task-oriented flagged-event representation applied e.g. in the ACE and BioNLP Shared Task evaluations. We presented a detailed manual analysis exploring points of disagreement and evaluated in detail rule-based and machine learning-based methods joining state-of-the-art systems representing the two approaches.

Our manual analysis identified a number of phenomena that limit the applicability of existing cue-and-scope based systems to the event extraction task, such as negation expressed through morphological change of words expressing events (e.g. *unphosphorylated*). To address these issues, we proposed a combination of heuristics and simple lexical features, carefully selected to address differences in perspective between the cue-and-scope and event-based frameworks and aiming to complement cue-and-scope analyses for creating task-oriented outputs.

To test our approach, we created a method suitable for use as a component of an event extraction pipeline that incorporates information from a previously proposed state-of-the-art cue-and-scope based negation/speculation detection system and a minimal set of features in an SVM-based system that was shown to enhance and in several cases improve upon the output of existing EE systems. Experiments on the BioNLP Shared Task 2011 EPI and ID datasets demonstrated that the combined approach could improve the results of the best-performing systems at the original task in 5 out of 6 cases, outperforming the highest results reported for any system for these two tasks.

There exist several potential targets for future work on improving our introduced system and to join cue-and-scope and event-based approaches. Since none of the existing EE corpora was constructed with the aim to solely cover negation and speculation annotations and taking into account our finding that merging datasets to compensate for data sparseness is beneficial, it might be worth considering other possible corpora or resources and how they can be used for training our machine learning system.

Also, it would be worthwhile to attempt to combine an existing EE system capable of detecting negation/speculation with our proposed method. Combining the two could yield an ensemble, improving upon an already strong system by bridging the differences in perspectives and tapping into the potential benefits of both approaches.

The system and all resources introduced in this work are publicly available for research purposes at: *https://github.com/ninjin/eepura*

Acknowledgements

The authors would like to thank the anonymous reviewers for their many insightful comments and suggestions for improvements.

This work was funded in part by UK Biotechnology and Biological Sciences Research Council (BBSRC) under project Automated Biological Event Extraction from the Literature for Drug Discovery (reference number: BB/G013160/1), by the Ministry of Education, Culture, Sports, Science and Technology of Japan under the Integrated Database Project and by the Swedish Royal Academy of Sciences.

References

Jari Björne and Tapio Salakoski. 2011. Generalizing Biomedical Event Extraction. In *Proceedings of the BioNLP 2011 Workshop Companion Volume for Shared Task*, pages 183–191.

Wendy W. Chapman, Will Bridewell, Paul Hanbury, Gregory F. Cooper, and Bruce G. Buchanan. 2001. A simple algorithm for identifying negated findings and diseases in discharge summaries. *Journal of biomedical informatics*, 34(5):301–310.

Rong-En Fan, Kai-Wei Chang, Cho-Jui Hsieh, Xiang-Rui Wang, and Chih-Jen Lin. 2008. LIBLINEAR: A Library for Large Linear Classification. *Journal of Machine Learning Research*, 9:1871–1874.

Richárd Farkas, Veronika Vincze, György Móra, János Csirik, and György Szarvas. 2010. The CoNLL-2010 Shared Task: Learning to Detect Hedges and their Scope in Natural Language Text. In *Proceedings of the Fourteenth Conference on Computational Natural Language Learning*, pages 1–12.

Carol Friedman, Philip O. Alderson, John H.M. Austin, James J. Cimino, and Stephen B. Johnson. 1994. A general natural-language text processor for clinical radiology. *Journal of the American Medical Informatics Association*, 1(2):161–174.

William R. Hersh. 1996. *Information retrieval: a health care perspective*. Springer.

Yuang Huang and Henry J. Lowe. 2007. A novel hybrid approach to automated negation detection in clinical radiology reports. *Journal of the American Medical Informatics Association*, 14(3):304–311.

Halil Kilicoglu and Sabine Bergler. 2010. A High-Precision Approach to Detecting Hedges and their Scopes. In *Proceedings of the Fourteenth Conference on Computational Natural Language Learning*, pages 70–77.

Halil Kilicoglu and Sabine Bergler. 2011. Adapting a General Semantic Interpretation Approach to Biological Event Extraction. In *Proceedings of the BioNLP 2011 Workshop Companion Volume for Shared Task*, pages 173–182.

Jin-Dong Kim, Tomoko Ohta, Sampo Pyysalo, Yoshinobu Kano, and Jun'ichi Tsujii. 2009. Overview of BioNLP'09 Shared Task on Event Extraction. In *Proceedings of the BioNLP 2009 Workshop Companion Volume for Shared Task*, pages 1–9.

Jin-Dong Kim, Sampo Pyysalo, Tomoko Ohta, Robert Bossy, Ngan Nguyen, and Jun'ichi Tsujii. 2011a. Overview of BioNLP Shared Task 2011. In *Proceedings of the BioNLP 2011 Workshop Companion Volume for Shared Task*, pages 1–6.

Jin-Dong Kim, Yue Wang, Toshihisa Takagi, and Akinori Yonezawa. 2011b. Overview of Genia Event Task in BioNLP Shared Task 2011. In *Proceedings of the BioNLP 2011 Workshop Companion Volume for Shared Task*, pages 7–15.

LDC. 2005. ACE (Automatic Content Extraction) English Annotation Guidelines for Events. Technical report, Linguistic Data Consortium.

David McClosky, Mihai Surdeanu, and Christopher Manning. 2011. Event Extraction as Dependency Parsing for BioNLP 2011. In *Proceedings of BioNLP 2011*, pages 41–45.

Roser Morante and Walter Daelemans. 2009. Learning the scope of hedge cues in biomedical texts. In *Proceedings of the Workshop on Current Trends in Biomedical Natural Language Processing*, pages 28–36.

Roser Morante, Vincent Van Asch, and Walter Daelemans. 2010. Memory-based resolution of in-sentence scopes of hedge cues. In *Proceedings of the Fourteenth Conference on Computational Natural Language Learning — Shared Task*, CoNLL 2010: Shared Task, pages 40–47.

Tomoko Ohta, Sampo Pyysalo, and Jun'ichi Tsujii. 2011. Overview of the Epigenetics and Post-translational Modifications (EPI) task of BioNLP Shared Task 2011. In *Proceedings of the BioNLP 2011 Workshop Companion Volume for Shared Task*, pages 16–25.

Sampo Pyysalo, Tomoko Ohta, Rafal Rak, Dan Sullivan, Chunhong Mao, Chunxia Wang, Bruno Sobral, Jun'ichi Tsujii, and Sophia Ananiadou. 2011. Overview of the Infectious Diseases (ID) task of BioNLP Shared Task 2011. In *Proceedings of the BioNLP 2011 Workshop Companion Volume for Shared Task*, pages 26–35.

Sampo Pyysalo, Pontus Stenetorp, Tomoka Ohta, Jin-Dong Kim, and Sophia Ananiadou. 2012. New Resources and Perspectives for Biomedical Event Extraction. In *Proceedings of BioNLP 2012 Workshop*. to appear.

Sebastian Riedel and Andrew McCallum. 2011. Robust Biomedical Event Extraction with Dual Decomposition and Minimal Domain Adaptation. In *Proceedings of the BioNLP 2011 Workshop Companion Volume for Shared Task*, pages 46–50.

Sebastian Riedel, David McClosky, Mihai Surdeanu, Andrew McCallum, and Christopher D. Manning. 2011. Model Combination for Event Extraction in BioNLP 2011. In *Proceedings of the BioNLP 2011 Workshop Companion Volume for Shared Task*, pages 51–55.

Roser Saur and James Pustejovsky. 2009. FactBank: a corpus annotated with event factuality. *Language Resources and Evaluation*, 43:227–268. 10.1007/s10579-009-9089-9.

Pontus Stenetorp, Goran Topić, Sampo Pyysalo, Tomoko Ohta, Jin-Dong Kim, and Jun'ichi Tsujii. 2011. BioNLP Shared Task 2011: Supporting Resources. In *Proceedings of the BioNLP 2011 Workshop Companion Volume for Shared Task*, pages 112–120.

Paul Thompson, Raheel Nawaz, John McNaught, and Sophia Ananiadou. 2011. Enriching a biomedical event corpus with meta-knowledge annotation. *BMC Bioinformatics*, 12(1):393.

Veronika Vincze, Gyorgy Szarvas, Richard Farkas, Gyorgy Mora, and Janos Csirik. 2008. The Bio-

Scope corpus: biomedical texts annotated for uncertainty, negation and their scopes. *BMC Bioinformatics*, 9(Suppl 11):S9.

Veronika Vincze, Gyorgy Szarvas, Gyorgy Mora, Tomoko Ohta, and Richard Farkas. 2011. Linguistic scope-based and biological event-based speculation and negation annotations in the BioScope and Genia Event corpora. *Journal of Biomedical Semantics*, 2(Suppl 5):S8.

Statistical Modality Tagging from Rule-based Annotations and Crowdsourcing

Vinodkumar Prabhakaran
CS
Columbia University
vinod@cs.columbia.edu

Michael Bloodgood
CASL
University of Maryland
meb@umd.edu

Mona Diab
CCLS
Columbia University
mdiab@ccls.columbia.edu

Bonnie Dorr
CS and UMIACS
University of Maryland
bonnie@umiacs.umd.edu

Lori Levin
LTI
Carnegie Mellon University
lsl@cs.cmu.edu

Christine D. Piatko
APL
Johns Hopkins University
christine.piatko@jhuapl.edu

Owen Rambow
CCLS
Columbia University
rambow@ccls.columbia.edu

Benjamin Van Durme
HLTCOE
Johns Hopkins University
vandurme@cs.jhu.edu

Abstract

We explore training an automatic modality tagger. Modality is the attitude that a speaker might have toward an event or state. One of the main hurdles for training a linguistic tagger is gathering training data. This is particularly problematic for training a tagger for modality because modality triggers are sparse for the overwhelming majority of sentences. We investigate an approach to automatically training a modality tagger where we first gathered sentences based on a high-recall simple rule-based modality tagger and then provided these sentences to Mechanical Turk annotators for further annotation. We used the resulting set of training data to train a precise modality tagger using a multi-class SVM that delivers good performance.

1 Introduction

Modality is an extra-propositional component of meaning. In *John may go to NY*, the basic proposition is *John go to NY* and the word *may* indicates modality. Van Der Auwera and Ammann (2005) define core cases of modality: *John must go to NY* (epistemic necessity), *John might go to NY* (epistemic possibility), *John has to leave now* (deontic necessity) and *John may leave now* (deontic possibility). Many semanticists (e.g. Kratzer (1981), Kratzer (1991), Kaufmann et al. (2006)) define modality as quantification over possible worlds. *John might go* means that there exist some possible worlds in which John goes. Another view of modality relates more to a speakers attitude toward a proposition (e.g. McShane et al. (2004)).

Modality might be construed broadly to include several types of attitudes that a speaker wants to express towards an event, state or proposition. Modality might indicate factivity, evidentiality, or sentiment (McShane et al., 2004). Factivity is related to whether the speaker wishes to convey his or her belief that the propositional content is true or not, i.e., whether it actually obtains in this world or not. It distinguishes things that (the speaker believes) happened from things that he or she desires, plans, or considers merely probable. Evidentiality deals with the source of information and may provide clues to the reliability of the information. Did the speaker have firsthand knowledge of what he or she is reporting, or was it hearsay or inferred from indirect evidence? Sentiment deals with a speaker's positive or negative feelings toward an event, state, or proposition.

In this paper, we focus on the following five modalities; we have investigated the belief/factivity modality previously (Diab et al., 2009b; Prabhakaran et al., 2010), and we leave other modalities to future work.

- **Ability:** can H do P?
- **Effort:** does H try to do P?
- **Intention:** does H intend P?
- **Success:** does H succeed in P?
- **Want:** does H want P?

We investigate automatically training a modality tagger by using multi-class Support Vector Machines (SVMs). One of the main hurdles for training a linguistic tagger is gathering training data. This is particularly problematic for training a modality tagger because modality triggers are sparse for the overwhelming majority of the sentences. Baker et al. (2010) created a modality tagger by using a semi-automatic approach for creating rules for a rule-based tagger. A pilot study revealed that it can boost recall well above the naturally occurring proportion of modality without annotated data but with only 60% precision. We investigated an approach where we first gathered sentences based on a simple modality tagger and then provided these sentences to annotators for further annotation, The resulting annotated data also preserved the level of inter-annotator agreement for each example so that learning algorithms could take that into account during training. Finally, the resulting set of annotations was used for training a modality tagger using SVMs, which gave a high precision indicating the success of this approach.

Section 2 discusses related work. Section 3 discusses our procedure for gathering training data. Section 4 discusses the machine learning setup and features used to train our modality tagger and presents experiments and results. Section 5 concludes and discusses future work.

2 Related Work

Previous related work includes TimeML (Sauri et al., 2006), which involves modality annotation on events, and Factbank (Sauri and Pustejovsky, 2009), where event mentions are marked with degree of factuality. Modality is also important in the detection of uncertainty and hedging. The CoNLL shared task in 2010 (Farkas et al., 2010) deals with automatic detection of uncertainty and hedging in Wikipedia and biomedical sentences.

Baker et al. (2010) and Baker et al. (2012) analyze a set of eight modalities which include belief, require and permit, in addition to the five modalities we focus on in this paper. They built a rule-based modality tagger using a semi-automatic approach to create rules. This earlier work differs from the work described in this paper in that the our emphasis is on the creation of an *automatic* modality tagger using machine learning techniques. Note that the annotation and automatic tagging of the belief modality (i.e., factivity) is described in more detail in (Diab et al., 2009b; Prabhakaran et al., 2010).

There has been a considerable amount of interest in modality in the biomedical domain. Negation, uncertainty, and hedging are annotated in the Bioscope corpus (Vincze et al., 2008), along with information about which words are in the scope of negation/uncertainty. The i2b2 NLP Shared Task in 2010 included a track for detecting assertion status (e.g. present, absent, possible, conditional, hypothetical etc.) of medical problems in clinical records.[1] Apostolova et al. (2011) presents a rule-based system for the detection of negation and speculation scopes using the Bioscope corpus. Other studies emphasize the importance of detecting uncertainty in medical text summarization (Morante and Daelemans, 2009; Aramaki et al., 2009).

Modality has also received some attention in the context of certain applications. Earlier work describing the difficulty of correctly translating modality using machine translation includes (Sigurd and Gawrónska, 1994) and (Murata et al., 2005). Sigurd et al. (1994) write about rule based frameworks and how using alternate grammatical constructions such as the passive can improve the rendering of the modal in the target language. Murata et al. (2005)

[1]https://www.i2b2.org/NLP/Relations/

analyze the translation of Japanese into English by several systems, showing they often render the present incorrectly as the progressive. The authors trained a support vector machine to specifically handle modal constructions, while our modal annotation approach is a part of a full translation system.

The textual entailment literature includes modality annotation schemes. Identifying modalities is important to determine whether a text entails a hypothesis. Bar-Haim et al. (2007) include polarity based rules and negation and modality annotation rules. The polarity rules are based on an independent polarity lexicon (Nairn et al., 2006). The annotation rules for negation and modality of predicates are based on identifying modal verbs, as well as conditional sentences and modal adverbials. The authors read the modality off parse trees directly using simple structural rules for modifiers.

3 Constructing Modality Training Data

In this section, we will discuss the procedure we followed to construct the training data for building the automatic modality tagger. In a pilot study, we obtained and ran the modality tagger described in (Baker et al., 2010) on the English side of the Urdu-English LDC language pack.[2] We randomly selected 1997 sentences that the tagger had labeled as not having the Want modality and posted them on Amazon Mechanical Turk (MTurk). Three different Turkers (MTurk annotators) marked, for each of the sentences, whether it contained the Want modality. Using majority rules as the Turker judgment, 95 (i.e., 4.76%) of these sentences were marked as having a Want modality. We also posted 1993 sentences that the tagger had labeled as having a Want modality and only 1238 of them were marked by the Turkers as having a Want modality. Therefore, the estimated precision of this type of approach is only around 60%.

Hence, we will not be able to use the (Baker et al., 2010) tagger to gather training data. Instead, our approach was to apply a simple tagger as a first pass, with positive examples subsequently hand-annotated using MTurk. We made use of sentence data from the Enron email corpus,[3] derived from the version owing to Fiore and Heer,[4] further processed as described by (Roark, 2009).[5]

To construct the simple tagger (the first pass), we used a lexicon of modality trigger words (e.g., *try, plan, aim, wish, want*) constructed by Baker et al. (2010). The tagger essentially tags each sentence that has a word in the lexicon with the corresponding modality. We wrote a few simple obvious filters for a handful of exceptional cases that arise due to the fact that our sentences are from e-mail. For example, we filtered out *best wishes* expressions, which otherwise would have been tagged as *Want* because of the word *wishes*.

The words that trigger modality occur with very different frequencies. If one is not careful, the training data may be dominated by only the commonly occurring trigger words and the learned tagger would then be biased towards these words. In order to ensure that our training data had a diverse set of examples containing many lexical triggers and not just a lot of examples with the same lexical trigger, for each modality we capped the number of sentences from a single trigger to be at most 50. After we had the set of sentences selected by the simple tagger, we posted them on MTurk for annotation.

The Turkers were asked to check a box indicating that the modality was not present in the sentence if the given modality was not expressed. If they did not check that box, then they were asked to highlight the target of the modality. Table 1 shows the number of sentences we posted on MTurk for each modality.[6] Three Turkers annotated each sentence. We restricted the task to Turkers who were adults, had greater than a 95% approval rating, and had completed at least 50 HITs (Human Intelligence Tasks) on MTurk. We paid US$0.10 for each set of ten sentences.

Since our data was annotated by three Turkers, for training data we used only those examples for which at least two Turkers agreed on the modality and the target of the modality. This resulted in 1,008 examples. 674 examples had two Turkers agreeing and 334 had unanimous agreement. We kept track of the level of agreement for each example so that

[2]LDC Catalog No.: LDC2006E110.

[3]http://www-2.cs.cmu.edu/~enron/

[4]http://bailando.sims.berkeley.edu/enron/enron.sql.gz

[5]Data received through personal communication

[6]More detailed statistics on MTurk annotations are available at http://hltcoe.jhu.edu/datasets/.

Modality	Count
Ability	190
Effort	1350
Intention	1320
Success	1160
Want	1390

Table 1: For each modality, the number of sentences returned by the simple tagger that we posted on MTurk.

Modality	MTurk	Gold
Ability	6%	48%
Effort	25%	10%
Intention	30%	11%
Success	24%	9%
Want	15%	23%

Table 2: Frequency of Modalities

our learner could weight the examples differently depending on the level of inter-annotator agreement.

4 Multiclass SVM for Modality

In this section, we describe the automatic modality tagger we built using the MTurk annotations described in Section 3 as the training data. Section 4.1 describes the training and evaluation data. In Section 4.2, we present the machinery and Section 4.3 describes the features we used to train the tagger. In Section 4.4, we present various experiments and discuss results. Section 4.5, presents additional experiments using annotator confidence.

4.1 Data

For training, we used the data presented in Section 3. We refer to it as MTurk data in the rest of this paper. For evaluation, we selected a part of the LU Corpus (Diab et al., 2009a) (1228 sentences) and our expert annotated it with modality tags. We first used the high-recall simple modality tagger described in Section 3 to select the sentences with modalities. Out of the 235 sentences returned by the simple modality tagger, our expert removed the ones which did not in fact have a modality. In the remaining sentences (94 sentences), our expert annotated the target predicate. We refer to this as the Gold dataset in this paper. The MTurk and Gold datasets differ in terms of genres as well as annotators (Turker vs. Expert). The distribution of modalities in both MTurk and Gold annotations are given in Table 2.

4.2 Approach

We applied a supervised learning framework using multi-class SVMs to automatically learn to tag modalities in context. For tagging, we used the Yamcha (Kudo and Matsumoto, 2003) sequence labeling system which uses the $\text{SVM}^{\text{light}}$ (Joachims, 1999) package for classification. We used *One versus All* method for multi-class classification on a quadratic kernel with a C value of 1. We report recall and precision on word tokens in our corpus for each modality. We also report $F_{\beta=1}$ (F)-measure as the harmonic mean between (P)recision and (R)ecall.

4.3 Features

We used lexical features at the token level which can be extracted without any parsing with relatively high accuracy. We use the term context width to denote the window of tokens whose features are considered for predicting the tag for a given token. For example, a context width of 2 means that the feature vector of any given token includes, in addition to its own features, those of 2 tokens before and after it as well as the tag prediction for 2 tokens before it. We did experiments varying the context width from 1 to 5 and found that a context width of 2 gives the optimal performance. All results reported in this paper are obtained with a context width of 2. For each token, we performed experiments using following lexical features:

- **wordStem** - Word stem.
- **wordLemma** - Word lemma.
- **POS** - Word's POS tag.
- **isNumeric** - Word is Numeric?
- **verbType** - Modal/Auxiliary/Regular/Nil
- **whichModal** - If the word is a modal verb, which modal?

We used the Porter stemmer (Porter, 1997) to obtain the stem of a word token. To determine the word lemma, we used an in-house lemmatizer using dictionary and morphological analysis to obtain the dictionary form of a word. We obtained POS tags from Stanford POS tagger and used those tags to determine *verbType* and *whichModal* features. The *verbType* feature is assigned a value 'Nil' if the word is not a verb and *whichModal* feature is assigned a value 'Nil' if the word is not a modal verb. The feature *isNumeric* is a binary feature denoting whether the token contains only digits or not.

4.4 Experiments and Results

In this section, we present experiments performed considering all the MTurk annotations where two annotators agreed and all the MTurk annotations where all three annotators agreed to be equally correct annotations. We present experiments applying differential weights for these annotations in Section 4.5. We performed 4-fold cross validation (4FCV) on MTurk data in order to select the best feature set configuration ϕ. The best feature set obtained was $wordStem, POS, whichModal$ with a context width of 2. For finding the best performing feature set - context width configuration, we did an exhaustive search on the feature space, pruning away features which were proven not useful by results at stages. Table 3 presents results obtained for each modality on 4-fold cross validation.

Modality	Precision	Recall	F Measure
Ability	82.4	55.5	65.5
Effort	95.1	82.8	88.5
Intention	84.3	61.3	70.7
Success	93.2	76.6	83.8
Want	88.4	64.3	74.3
Overall	**90.1**	**70.6**	**79.1**

Table 3: Per modality results for best feature set ϕ on 4-fold cross validation on MTurk data

We also trained a model on the entire MTurk data using the best feature set ϕ and evaluated it against the Gold data. The results obtained for each modality on gold evaluation are given in Table 4. We attribute the lower performance on the Gold dataset to its difference from MTurk data. MTurk data is entirely from email threads, whereas Gold data contained sentences from newswire, letters and blogs in addition to emails. Furthermore, the annotation is different (Turkers vs expert). Finally, the distribution of modalities in both datasets is very different. For example, *Ability* modality was merely 6% of MTurk data compared to 48% in Gold data (see Table 2).

Modality	Precision	Recall	F Measure
Ability	78.6	22.0	34.4
Effort	85.7	60.0	70.6
Intention	66.7	16.7	26.7
Success	NA	0.0	NA
Want	92.3	50.0	64.9
Overall	**72.1**	**29.5**	**41.9**

Table 4: Per modality results for best feature set ϕ evaluated on Gold dataset

We obtained reasonable performances for *Effort* and *Want* modalities while the performance for other modalities was rather low. Also, the Gold dataset contained only 8 instances of *Success*, none of which was recognized by the tagger resulting in a recall of 0%. Precision (and, accordingly, F Measure) for *Success* was considered "not applicable" (NA), as no such tag was assigned.

4.5 Annotation Confidence Experiments

Our MTurk data contains sentence for which at least two of the three Turkers agreed on the modality and the target of the modality. In this section, we investigate the role of annotation confidence in training an automatic tagger. The annotation confidence is denoted by whether an annotation was agreed by only two annotators or was unanimous. We denote the set of sentences for which only two annotators agreed as Agr_2 and that for which all three annotators agreed as Agr_3.

We present four training setups. The first setup is $Tr23$ where we train a model using both Agr_2 and Agr_3 with equal weights. This is the setup we used for results presented in the Section 4.4. Then, we have $Tr2$ and $Tr3$, where we train using only Agr_2 and Agr_3 respectively. Then, for $Tr23_W$, we

TrainingSetup	Tested on Agr_2 and Agr_3			Tested on Agr_3 only		
	Precision	Recall	F Measure	Precision	Recall	F Measure
$Tr23$	90.1	**70.6**	**79.1**	95.9	**86.8**	**91.1**
$Tr2$	**91.0**	66.1	76.5	95.6	81.8	88.2
$Tr3$	88.1	52.3	65.6	**96.8**	71.7	82.3
$Tr23_W$	89.9	70.5	79.0	95.8	86.5	90.9

Table 5: Annotator Confidence Experiment Results; the best results per column are boldfaced (4-fold cross validation on MTurk Data)

train a model giving different cost values for Agr_2 and Agr_3 examples. The SVMLight package allows users to input cost values c_i for each training instance separately.[7] We tuned this cost value for Agr_2 and Agr_3 examples and found the best value at 20 and 30 respectively.

For all four setups, we used feature set ϕ. We performed 4-fold cross validation on MTurk data in two ways — we tested against a combination of Agr_2 and Agr_3, and we tested against only Agr_3. Results of these experiments are presented in Table 5. We also present the results of evaluating a tagger trained on the whole MTurk data for each setup against the Gold annotation in Table 6. The $Tr23$ tested on both Agr_2 and Agr_3 presented in Table 5 and $Tr23$ tested on Gold data presented in Table 6 correspond to the results presented in Table 3 and Table 4 respectively.

TrainingSetup	Precision	Recall	F Measure
$Tr23$	72.1	29.5	41.9
$Tr2$	67.4	27.6	39.2
$Tr3$	**74.1**	19.1	30.3
$Tr23_W$	73.3	**31.4**	**44.0**

Table 6: Annotator Confidence Experiment Results; the best results per column are boldfaced (Evaluation against Gold)

One main observation is that including annotations of lower agreement, but still above a threshold (in our case, 66.7%), is definitely helpful. $Tr23$ outperformed both $Tr2$ and $Tr3$ in both recall and F-measure in all evaluations. Also, even when evaluating against only the high confident Agr_3 cases, $Tr2$ gave a high gain in recall (10 .1 percentage points) over $Tr3$, with only a 1.2 percentage point loss on precision. We conjecture that this is because there are far more training instances in $Tr2$ than in $Tr3$ (674 vs 334), and that quantity beats quality.

Another important observation is the increase in performance by using varied costs for Agr_2 and Agr_3 examples (the $Tr23_W$ condition). Although it dropped the performance by 0.1 to 0.2 points in cross-validation F measure on the Enron corpora, it gained 2.1 points in Gold evaluation F measure. These results seem to indicate that differential weighting based on annotator agreement might have more beneficial impact when training a model that will be applied to a wide range of genres than when training a model with genre-specific data for application to data from the same genre. Put differently, using varied costs prevents genre over-fitting. We don't have a full explanation for this difference in behavior yet. We plan to explore this in future work.

5 Conclusion

We have presented an innovative way of combining a high-recall simple tagger with Mechanical Turk annotations to produce training data for a modality tagger. We show that we obtain good performance on the same genre as this training corpus (annotated in the same manner), and reasonable performance across genres (annotated by an independent expert). We also present experiments utilizing the number of agreeing Turkers to choose cost values for training examples for the SVM. As future work, we plan to extend this approach to other modalities which are

[7]This can be done by specifying 'cost:<value>' after the label in each training instance. This feature has not yet been documented on the SVMlight website.

not covered in this study.

6 Acknowledgments

This work is supported, in part, by the Johns Hopkins Human Language Technology Center of Excellence. Any opinions, findings, and conclusions or recommendations expressed in this material are those of the authors and do not necessarily reflect the views of the sponsor. We thank several anonymous reviewers for their constructive feedback.

References

Emilia Apostolova, Noriko Tomuro, and Dina Demner-Fushman. 2011. Automatic extraction of lexico-syntactic patterns for detection of negation and speculation scopes. In *Proceedings of the 49th Annual Meeting of the Association for Computational Linguistics: Human Language Technologies: short papers - Volume 2*, HLT '11, pages 283–287, Portland, Oregon.

Eiji Aramaki, Yasuhide Miura, Masatsugu Tonoike, Tomoko Ohkuma, Hiroshi Mashuichi, and Kazuhiko Ohe. 2009. Text2table: Medical text summarization system based on named entity recognition and modality identification. In *Proceedings of the BioNLP 2009 Workshop*, pages 185–192, Boulder, Colorado, June. Association for Computational Linguistics.

Kathryn Baker, Michael Bloodgood, Bonnie J. Dorr, Nathaniel W. Filardo, Lori S. Levin, and Christine D. Piatko. 2010. A modality lexicon and its use in automatic tagging. In *LREC*.

Kathryn Baker, Michael Bloodgood, Bonnie J. Dorr, Chris Callison-Burch, Nathaniel W. Filardo, Christine Piatko, Lori Levin, and Scott Miller. 2012. Use of modality and negation in semantically-informed syntactic mt. *Computational Linguistics*, 38(22).

Roy Bar-Haim, Ido Dagan, Iddo Greental, and Eyal Shnarch. 2007. Semantic inference at the lexical-syntactic level. In *Proceedings of the 22nd National Conference on Artificial intelligence - Volume 1*, pages 871–876, Vancouver, British Columbia, Canada. AAAI Press.

Mona Diab, Bonnie Dorr, Lori Levin, Teruko Mitamura, Rebecca Passonneau, Owen Rambow, and Lance Ramshaw. 2009a. *Language Understanding Annotation Corpus*. Linguistic Data Consortium (LDC), USA.

Mona Diab, Lori Levin, Teruko Mitamura, Owen Rambow, Vinodkumar Prabhakaran, and Weiwei Guo. 2009b. Committed belief annotation and tagging. In *Proceedings of the Third Linguistic Annotation Workshop*, pages 68–73, Suntec, Singapore, August. Association for Computational Linguistics.

Richárd Farkas, Veronika Vincze, György Szarvas, György Móra, and János Csirik, editors. 2010. *Proceedings of the Fourteenth Conference on Computational Natural Language Learning*. Association for Computational Linguistics, Uppsala, Sweden, July.

Thorsten Joachims, 1999. *Making large-scale support vector machine learning practical*, pages 169–184. MIT Press, Cambridge, MA, USA.

Stefan Kaufmann, Cleo Condoravdi, and Valentina Harizanov, 2006. *Formal Approaches to Modality*, pages 72–106. Mouton de Gruyter.

Angelika Kratzer. 1981. The Notional Category of Modality. In H. J. Eikmeyer and H. Rieser, editors, *Words, Worlds, and Contexts*, pages 38–74. de Gruyter, Berlin.

Angelika Kratzer. 1991. Modality. In Arnim von Stechow and Dieter Wunderlich, editors, *Semantics: An International Handbook of Contemporary Research*. de Gruyter.

Taku Kudo and Yuji Matsumoto. 2003. Fast methods for kernel-based text analysis. In *41st Meeting of the Association for Computational Linguistics (ACL'03)*, Sapporo, Japan.

Marjorie McShane, Sergei Nirenburg, and Ron Zacharsky. 2004. Mood and modality: Out of the theory and into the fray. *Natural Language Engineering*, 19(1):57–89.

Roser Morante and Walter Daelemans. 2009. Learning the scope of hedge cues in biomedical texts. In *Proceedings of the BioNLP 2009 Workshop*, pages 28–36, Boulder, Colorado, June. Association for Computational Linguistics.

Masaki Murata, Kiyotaka Uchimoto, Qing Ma, Toshiyuki Kanamaru, and Hitoshi Isahara. 2005. Analysis of machine translation systems' errors in tense, aspect, and modality. In *Proceedings of the 19th Asia-Pacific Conference on Language, Information and Computation (PACLIC)*, Tapei.

Rowan Nairn, Cleo Condorovdi, and Lauri Karttunen. 2006. Computing relative polarity for textual inference. In *Proceedings of the International Workshop on Inference in Computational Semantics*, ICoS-5, pages 66–76, Buxton, England.

M. F. Porter, 1997. *An algorithm for suffix stripping*, pages 313–316. Morgan Kaufmann Publishers Inc., San Francisco, CA, USA.

Vinodkumar Prabhakaran, Owen Rambow, and Mona Diab. 2010. Automatic committed belief tagging. In *Coling 2010: Posters*, pages 1014–1022, Beijing, China, August. Coling 2010 Organizing Committee.

Brian Roark. 2009. Open vocabulary language modeling for binary response typing interfaces. Technical report, Oregon Health and Science University.

Roser Sauri and James Pustejovsky. 2009. Factbank: a corpus annotated with event factuality. *Language Resources and Evaluation*, 43(3):227–268.

Roser Sauri, Marc Verhagen, and James Pustejovsky. 2006. Annotating and recognizing event modality in text. In *FLAIRS Conference*, pages 333–339.

Bengt Sigurd and Barbara Gawrónska. 1994. Modals as a problem for MT. In *Proceedings of the 15th International Conference on Computational Linguistics (COLING) Volume 1*, COLING '94, pages 120–124, Kyoto, Japan.

Johan Van Der Auwera and Andreas Ammann, 2005. *Overlap between situational and epistemic modal marking*, chapter 76, pages 310–313. Oxford University Press.

Veronika Vincze, Gy orgy Szarvas, Richád Farkas, Gy orgy Mora, and János Csirik. 2008. The BioScope corpus: biomedical texts annotated for uncertainty, negation and their scopes. *BMC Bioinformatics*, 9(Suppl 11):S9+.

Annotating the Focus of Negation in terms of Questions Under Discussion

Pranav Anand
Department of Linguistics
University of California, Santa Cruz
Santa Cruz, CA 95064 USA
panand@ucsc.edu

Craig Martell
Department of Computer Science
Naval Postgraduate School
Monterey, CA USA
cmartell@nps.edu

Abstract

Blanco & Moldovan (Blanco and Moldovan, 2011) have empirically demonstrated that negated sentences often convey implicit positive inferences, or focus, and that these inferences are both human annotatable and machine learnable. Concentrating on their annotation process, this paper argues that the focus-based implicit positivity should be separated from concepts of scalar implicature and neg-raising, as well as the placement of stress. We show that a model making these distinctions clear and which incorporates the pragmatic notion of question under discussion yields κ rates above .80, but that it substantially deflates the rates of focus of negation in text.

1 Introduction

The recent paper by Blanco & Moldovan (Blanco and Moldovan, 2011) has highlighted the fact that negation in natural language is more that just a propositional logic operator. The central claims of the paper are that negation conveys implicit positivity more than half of the time and that such positivity is both reliably annotatable by humans and promisingly learnable by machine. In this paper, we evaluate their annotation process and propose a different model that incorporates the pragmatic concept that discourse is guided by *questions under discussion* (QUDs), often implicit issues that hearers and speakers are attending to. We concentrate on the corpus used in (Blanco and Moldovan, 2011), PB-FOC.[1]

Our animating concern can be seen concretely by comparing the examples[2] from the corpus provided below.

(1) a. "They were willing to mistreat us because we hadn't shown **any moxie, any resistance**," says William Queenan, a DC-10 pilot and 14-year Federal veteran. (ex. 939)

b. "**I** won't be throwing *90 mph*, but I will throw 80-plus," he says. (ex. 1)

c. "**Some shows** just don't impress, he says, and this is one of them." (ex. 30)

d. "But we don't believe **there is enough of a difference to be clinically significant**," Dr. Sobel said. (ex. 426)

We believe these examples are incorrectly annotated, but in somewhat different ways. Following Blanco & Moldovan, assume that focus of negation is diagnosed by an implication that some alternative to the focus would make a sentence true. Then in (1a), in which the focus is annotated as being on the negative polarity item *any moxie, any resistance*, it is not clear that there is focus at all. If there were, the sentence would imply that the pilots in question showed something but not some moxie. This doesn't seem to be the meaning intended. In contrast, in (1b), we agree that focus is present, but take it to be on the phrase *90 mph*, as is confirmed

[1] PB-FOC was released as part of **SEM 2012 Shared Task: Resolving the Scope and Focus of Negation* http://www.clips.ua.ac.be/sem2012-st-neg/

[2] The citation (ex. n) will refer to the nth annotated instance in the PB-FOC dataset. In these and following examples, we indicate the PB-FOC focus by emboldening and our suggested alternative (if present) by italics

by the overt contrast that follows. Finally, (1c) and (1d) both show something more complex; in (1c) the scalar quantifier *some* is not in the scope of negation (lest it mean no shows impress), and thus cannot be a focus. Nonetheless, we agree that a positive implicature arises here (namely, that some shows do impress), but we suggest that this is simply a fact about scalar implicatures. Finally, in (1d), in which the verb *believe* is a so-called neg-raiser (a predicate P such that $\neg P(x) \leftrightarrow P(\neg x)$), the implicit positivity about a belief the doctors have is not due to pragmatic focus, but a lexical property of the verb in question.

In sum, what worried us was the variety of constructions being considered equivalent. In order to respond to these concerns, we reannotated 2304 sentences from the development subcorpus, being careful to try to tease apart the relevant distinctions mentioned above. This paper documents that effort. Our central finding is that the PB-FOC data contains an overabundance of focus-marked phrases (i.e., cases like (1a)): the PB-FOC rate of focus marking in our subcorpus is 74% (somewhat higher than the 65% for the whole dataset), while we observed a rate of 50%. Although the reduction in focus-marking occurs across all Propbank role types, we show that it is highest with the A1 and AM-MNR roles. One central reason for the overmarking, we argue, is that the definition of focus of negation Blanco & Moldovan use is somewhat vague, allowing one to confuse emphasis with implicit positivity. We argue instead that although they are right to correlate stress with focus (by and large), focus is connected to referencing a QUD (Rooth, 1996; Roberts, 1996; Kadmon, 2001), and only indirectly leads to positivity.

2 Delimiting Focus of Negation

2.1 What Focus of Negation is

Following (Huddleston and Pullman, 2002), Blanco & Moldovan define the focus of negation as "that part of the scope [of negation] that is most prominently or explicitly negated." They further argue that when there is a focus of negation, it yields a corresponding positive inference. This idea has roots in Jackendoff's seminal theory of focus (Jackendoff, 1972). Jackendoff proposes a) that focus in general (with or without negation) partitions a sentence into a function, obtained by lambda abstracting over the focused constituent and b) that negation is a focus-sensitive operator, stating that the function applied to the focused constituent yields falsity. To capture the positive inference cases, Jackendoff initially claims that focus always presupposes that there is some element in the function's domain (i.e., there is some way to make the sentence true).

(2) Bill likes **Mary**. $\mapsto \langle \lambda x$ Bill likes x, Mary$\rangle$

(3) not($\langle f, x\rangle$) = 0.

(4) focus presupposition: $\exists y[f(y) = 1]$.

While 4 might be correct for focus-sensitive operators like *only*, it is clearly not for negation. As Jackendoff himself points out, the sentence

(5) Bill doesn't like **anybody**.

clearly does not lead to the inference that Bill likes someone, even when *anybody* is strongly stressed. More contemporary work (Rooth, 1996; Roberts, 1996) has instead argued that what focus presupposes is that there is a relevant question under discussion (QUD). In the case of 2, it is the question

(6) Who does Bill like?

The QUD model assumes that dialogue is structured in terms of currently relevant (often implicit) questions, which serve to explain how a coherent discourse arises. Focus is thus coherent in context if the corresponding QUD is relevant. This serves to explain Jackendoff's counterexample (5) – *anybody* is focused because the question (6) is currently relevant. Under this account, focus of negation does not automatically yield an existential positive inference, but only if the corresponding QUD is assumed to exclude negative answers (i.e., if it is assumed that *no one* is not a suitable answer to *Who does Bill like?*). Adopting the QUD model thus means that in determining the positive inferences from a negated sentence, we must ask two questions:

a) What is the relevant QUD for this sentence/subsentence?

b) Does that QUD in context prohibit negative answers?

2.2 What isn't Focus of Negation

Thus, we see that the positive inference resulting from a negated sentence is the result of an interplay of the general meaning of focus (referencing a relevant QUD) and context (furnishing an assumption that some non-negative answer to the QUD exists). However, there is another way of yielding positive inferences to negated sentences, relying merely on the familiar theory of scalar implicature. Consider (7) below, which involves the scalar expression *much* (roughly equivalent to *a lot*). In positive assertions, using the quantifier *a lot* entails the corresponding alternative with *some*, and using *all* entails *a lot*. In the scope of negation, these patterns reverse, giving rise to opposite implicatures. Thus, (7) implicates that the stronger alternative (8) is false and thus (9) – that *some but not much* of a clue is given.

(7) assertion: However, it doesn't give much of a clue as to whether a recession is on the horizon. (ex. 122)

(8) stronger alternative: It doesn't give any clue as to whether a recession is on the horizon.

(9) implicature: It gives some clue as to whether the recession is on the horizon.

A different problem occurs with 'neg-raising' predicates like *believe, expect, think, seem,* and *want*. Since (Filmore, 1963), it has been noted that some clausal embedding predicates seem to interpret a superordinate negation inside their scope – that is, BILL DOESN'T THINK MARY IS HERE seems to be equivalent to BILL THINKS MARY ISN'T HERE.

While neg-raising is defeasible in certain contexts and its explanation is contentious (see (Gajewski, 2007) for discussion), it does not seem to be dependent on focus *per se*. In particular, putting focus on any element in the complement clause seems to engender a different positive inference. For example, in (10), this would give rise to the inference that Bill wants to talk to someone else, not simply that he wants to not talk to Mary.

(10) Bill doesn't want to talk to **Mary**.

In short, neg-raising cases should be considered more properly to be cases where the *scope* of negation is semantically lower than it appears, not cases of focus driven inference.

3 Reannotation

We annotated 2304 examples from the shared task training corpus. As in the original study, annotators were shown a target sentence as well as the prior and following sentence and were asked to mark the focus of negation in the target. Annotators followed a three step process. First, they were instructed to "move" the negation around the sentence to various constituents, as exemplified below, introducing an existential quantificational *some... but not*.

(11) a. $[\text{She}]_{A0}$ didn't have $[\text{hot water}]_{A1}$ $[\textbf{for five days}]_{AM-TMP}$. (ex. 1925)

b. Someone but not her had hot water for five days.

c. She had something but not hot water for five days.

d. She had hot water but not for five days.

They were then asked to determine which if any of these was most relevant, given the surrounding context and mark that as the focus. In determining which was most relevant, annotators asked whether the question corresponding to each altered sentence (e.g., Who had hot water for five days?) appeared to be under discussion in context.[3]

Three linguist annotators were selected and trained on 20 examples randomly drawn from the training set, including 5 examples of scalar "focus", 3 of neg-raising, and 5 instances of no focus. Annotators were given explicit feedback on each trial annotated. The annotators then annotated the remaining 2284 examples in our subcorpus with 100% overlap and 2 annotators per token.

3.1 Results

Figure 1 summarizes the differences between PB-FOC and our annotation by role[4]. Our annotators achieved a pairwise κ of 0.82. Our agreement with PB-FOC was significantly lower: $\kappa = 0.48$ if we exclude scalars and neg-raisers and 0.59 if we count them as focused.

[3]The QUD model in general allows multiple foci, e.g., Who had hot water when? We did not consider multiple foci in the present study.

[4]*Other* consists of C-A1, AM-PNC, AM-LOC, A4, R-A1, AM-EXT, A3, R-A0, AM-DIR, AM-DIS, R-AM-LOC

PB-FOC ROLE	COUNT	AGREED	SCALAR	NEG-RAISING	NO FOCUS	OTHER
A1	920	332	54	101	372	61
NO FOCUS	591	532	0	0	AGREED	59
AM-TMP	160	116	0	0	29	15
AM-MNR	125	51	28	0	40	6
A2	112	43	1	0	47	21
A0	88	24	20	0	23	21
AM-ADV	77	30	3	0	26	18
No Role	69	42	2	0	19	6
Other	161	42	8	20	75	16
TOTAL	2303	1212	116	121	631	223

Figure 1: Overall comparison of roles

As Figure 1 shows, the central reason for this discrepancy is the 631 examples where our annotators did not find focus where PB-FOC indicated that there was some; in contrast, only 59 examples that PB-FOC labeled as focusless were disagreed with. There are two interesting trends. First, we found an abundance of cases where the the question produced by the PB-FOC focus yielded an uninformative question (12% of disagreements), often in cases containing predicates of possession (e.g., *have, contain*). For example, in (12), the PB-FOC label would be answer the question *What do American Brands conclude they have under the contract?*, which does not seem relevant in context.

(12) possession (7%): "We have previously had discussions with representatives of Pinkerton's Inc. concerning the (sale of the company) and we concluded that we did not have **liability** under the contract," says American Brands. (ex. 181)

An additional 4% of the disagreements involved idiomatic expressions, where neither the syntactic nor the semantic sub-constituents could be meaningfully separated; in (13), *take kindly to that* as a whole is negated, and focusing on any one part will upset the idiom. Although of small number, the biased questions exemplified in (14) are illustrative of negation's chimerical lives; in these questions, negation's function is at the discourse level and it has no propositional negative force.

(13) idioms (4%): But media-stock analyst Richard J. MacDonald of MacDonald Grippo Riely says Wall Street won't take **kindly** to that. (ex. 2081)

(14) biased questions (10 instances): But wouldn't a president who acted despite Senate objections be taking **grave political risks**? (ex. 489)

4 Conclusion

We have argued that while the study of the focus of negation is of compelling interest to the computational community, more work is needed at theory- and annotation-building levels before we can effectively ask machine learning questions. We have suggested that one promising route for pursuing this is to operationalize the question under discussion model of focus's contribution to a sentence, and that such a procedure yields a marked decrease in the prevalence of focus of negation in PB-FOC. This partly follows from our decision on linguistic grounds to separate focus of negation from scalar implicature and neg-raising. From an engineering perspective, if our goal is to extract any positive inference from negated clauses, such distinctions may be academic. We suspect, however, that the linguistic heterogeneity substantially complicates annotator's task. We have shown that by explicitly telling annotators what the differences are, agreement rises, and we think future work should incorporate such a model. Finally, we plan on annotating foci that do not yield positive inferences, since it has the hope of giving us a window into when and how focus gives rise to positivity.

References

Eduardo Blanco and Dan Moldovan. 2011. Semantic Representation of Negation Using Focus Detection. In *Proceedings of the 49th Annual Meeting of the Association for Computational Linguistics: Human Language Technologies (ACL-HLT 2011)*, Portland, OR, USA.

Charles Filmore. 1963. The position of embedding transformations in grammar. *Word*, 19:208–231.

Jan Robert Gajewski. 2007. Neg-raising and polarity. *Linguistics and Philosophy*, 30:289–328.

Rodney Huddleston and Geoffrey K. Pullman. 2002. *The Cambridge Grammar of the English Langauge*. Cambridge University Press.

Ray Jackendoff. 1972. *Semantic Interpretation in Generative Grammar*. MIT Press, Cambridge, Mass.

Nirit Kadmon. 2001. *Formal Pragmatics: Semantics, Pragmatics, Presupposition, and Focus*. Wiley-Blackwell.

Craige Roberts. 1996. Information structure: Towards an integrated theory of formal pragmatics. In Jae-Hak Yoon and Andreas Kathol, editors, *OSU Working Papers in Linguistics, Volume 49: Papers in Semantics*, pages 91–136. The Ohio State University Department of Linguistics.

Mats Rooth. 1996. Focus. In Shalom Lappin, editor, *The Handbook of Contemporary Semantic Theory*, pages 271–298. Blackwell, Oxford.

Hedge Detection as a Lens on Framing in the GMO Debates: A Position Paper

Eunsol Choi[*], **Chenhao Tan**[*], **Lillian Lee**[*], **Cristian Danescu-Niculescu-Mizil**[*] and **Jennifer Spindel**[†]
[*]Department of Computer Science, [†]Department of Plant Breeding and Genetics
Cornell University
ec472@cornell.edu, chenhao|llee|cristian@cs.cornell.edu, jes462@cornell.edu

Abstract

Understanding the ways in which participants in public discussions frame their arguments is important in understanding how public opinion is formed. In this paper, we adopt the position that it is time for more computationally-oriented research on problems involving framing. In the interests of furthering that goal, we propose the following specific, interesting and, we believe, relatively accessible question: In the controversy regarding the use of genetically-modified organisms (GMOs) in agriculture, do pro- and anti-GMO articles differ in whether they choose to adopt a more "scientific" tone?

Prior work on the rhetoric and sociology of science suggests that *hedging* may distinguish popular-science text from text written by professional scientists for their colleagues. We propose a detailed approach to studying whether hedge detection can be used to understanding scientific framing in the GMO debates, and provide corpora to facilitate this study. Some of our preliminary analyses suggest that hedges occur less frequently in scientific discourse than in popular text, a finding that contradicts prior assertions in the literature. We hope that our initial work and data will encourage others to pursue this promising line of inquiry.

1 Introduction

1.1 Framing, "scientific discourse", and GMOs in the media

The issue of *framing* (Goffman, 1974; Scheufele, 1999; Benford and Snow, 2000) is of great importance in understanding how public opinion is formed. In their *Annual Review of Political Science* survey, Chong and Druckman (2007) describe framing effects as occurring "when (often small) changes in the presentation of an issue or an event produce (sometimes large) changes of opinion" (p. 104); as an example, they cite a study wherein respondents answered differently, when asked whether a hate group should be allowed to hold a rally, depending on whether the question was phrased as one of "free speech" or one of "risk of violence".

The genesis of our work is in a framing question motivated by a relatively current political issue. In media coverage of transgenic crops and the use of genetically modified organisms (GMOs) in food, do pro-GMO vs. anti-GMO articles differ not just with respect to word choice, but in adopting a more "scientific" discourse, meaning the inclusion of more uncertainty and fewer emotionally-laden words? We view this as an interesting question from a text analysis perspective (with potential applications and implications that lie outside the scope of this article).

1.2 Hedging as a sign of scientific discourse

To obtain a computationally manageable characterization of "scientific discourse", we turned to studies of the culture and language of science, a body of work spanning fields ranging from sociology to applied linguistics to rhetoric and communication (Gilbert and Mulkay, 1984; Latour, 1987; Latour and Woolgar, 1979; Halliday and Martin, 1993; Bazerman, 1988; Fahnestock, 2004; Gross, 1990).

One characteristic that has drawn quite a bit of attention in such studies is *hedging* (Myers, 1989;

Hyland, 1998; Lewin, 1998; Salager-Meyer, 2011).[1] Hyland (1998, pg. 1) defines hedging as the expression of "tentativeness and possibility" in communication, or, to put it another way, language corresponding to "the writer withholding full commitment to statements" (pg. 3). He supplies many real-life examples from scientific research articles, including the following:

1. '*It seems that* this group plays a critical role in orienting the carboxyl function' (emphasis Hyland's)

2. '...*implies that* phytochrome A is also not necessary for normal photomorphogenesis, *at least under these irradiation conditions*' (emphasis Hyland's)

3. '*We wish to suggest* a structure for the salt of deoxyribose nucleic acid (D.N.A.)' (emphasis added)[2]

Several scholars have asserted the centrality of hedging in scientific and academic discourse, which corresponds nicely to the notion of "more uncertainty" mentioned above. Hyland (1998, p. 6) writes, "Despite a widely held belief that professional scientific writing is a series of impersonal statements of fact which add up to the truth, hedges are abundant in science and play a critical role in academic writing". Indeed, Myers (1989, p. 13) claims that in scientific research articles, "The hedging of claims is so common that a sentence that looks like a claim but has no hedging is probably not a statement of new knowledge".[3]

Not only is understanding hedges important to understanding the rhetoric and sociology of science, but hedge detection and analysis — in the sense of identifying uncertain or uncertainly-sourced information (Farkas et al., 2010) — has important applications to information extraction, broadly construed, and has thus become an active sub-area of natural-language processing. For example, the CoNLL 2010 Shared Task was devoted to this problem (Farkas et al., 2010).

Putting these two lines of research together, we see before us what appears to be an interesting interdisciplinary and, at least in principle, straightforward research program: relying on the aforementioned rhetoric analyses to presume that hedging is a key characteristic of scientific discourse, build a hedge-detection system to computationally ascertain which proponents in the GMO debate tend to use more hedges and thus, by presumption, tend to adopt a more "scientific" frame.[4]

1.3 Contributions

Our overarching goal in this paper is to convince more researchers in NLP and computational linguistics to work on problems involving framing. We try to do so by proposing a specific problem that may be relatively accessible. Despite the apparent difficulty in addressing such questions, we believe that progress can be made by drawing on observations drawn from previous literature across many fields, and integrating such work with movements in the computational community toward consideration of extra-propositional and pragmatic concerns. We have thus intentionally tried to "cover a lot of ground", as one referee put it, in the introductory material just discussed.

Since framing problems are indeed difficult, we elected to narrow our scope in the hope of making some partial progress. Our technical goal here, at this workshop, where hedge detection is one of the most relevant topics to the broad questions we have raised, is *not* to learn to classify texts as being pro- vs. anti-GMO, or as being scientific or not, per se.[5] Our focus is on whether hedging specifically, considered as a single feature, is correlated with these different document classes, because of the previous research attention that has been devoted to hedging in particular and because of hedging being one of the topics of this workshop. The point of this paper is

[1] In linguistics, hedging has been studied since the 1970s (Lakoff, 1973).

[2] This example originates from Watson and Crick's landmark 1953 paper. Although the sentence is overtly tentative, did Watson and Crick truly intend to be polite and modest in their claims? See Varttala (2001) for a review of arguments regarding this question.

[3] Note the inclusion of the hedge "probably".

[4] However, this presumption that more hedges characterize a more scientific discourse has been contested. See section 2 for discussion and section 4.2 for our empirical investigation.

[5] Several other groups have addressed the problem of trying to identify different sides or perspectives (Lin et al., 2006; Hardisty et al., 2010; Beigman Klebanov et al., 2010; Ahmed and Xing, 2010).

thus not to compare the efficacy of hedging features with other types, such as bag-of-words features. Of course, to do so is an important and interesting direction for future work.

In the end, we were not able to achieve satisfactory results even with respect to our narrowed goal. However, we believe that other researchers may be able to follow the plan of attack we outline below, and perhaps use the data we are releasing, in order to achieve our goal. We would welcome hearing the results of other people's efforts.

2 How should we test whether hedging distinguishes scientific text?

One very important point that we have not yet addressed is: While the literature agrees on the importance of hedging in scientific text, the *relative degree* of hedging in scientific vs. non-scientific text is a matter of debate.

On the one side, we have assertions like those of Fahnestock (1986), who shows in a clever, albeit small-scale, study involving parallel texts that when scientific observations pass into popular accounts, changes include "removing hedges ... thus conferring greater certainty on the reported facts" (pg. 275). Similarly, Juanillo, Jr. (2001) refers to a shift from a forensic style to a "celebratory" style when scientific research becomes publicized, and credits Brown (1998) with noting that "celebratory scientific discourses tend to pay less attention to caveats, contradictory evidence, and qualifications that are highlighted in forensic or empiricist discourses. By downplaying scientific uncertainty, it [sic] alludes to greater certainty of scientific results for public consumption" (Juanillo, Jr., 2001, p. 42).

However, others have contested claims that the popularization process involves simplification, distortion, hype, and dumbing down, as Myers (2003) colorfully puts it; he provides a critique of the relevant literature. Varttala (1999) ran a corpus analysis in which hedging was found not just in professional medical articles, but was also "typical of popular scientific articles dealing with similar topics" (p. 195). Moreover, significant variation in use of hedging has been found across disciplines and authors' native language; see Salager-Meyer (2011) or Varttala (2001) for a review.

To the best of our knowledge, there have been no large-scale empirical studies validating the hypothesis that hedges appear more or less frequently in scientific discourse.

Proposed procedure Given the above, our **first step** must be to determine whether hedges are more or less prominent in "professional scientific" (henceforth "*prof-science*") vs. "public science" (henceforth "*pop-science*") discussions of GMOs. Of course, for a large-scale study, finding hedges requires developing and training an effective hedge detection algorithm.

If the first step shows that hedges can indeed be used to effectively distinguish prof-science vs. pop-science discourse on GMOs, then the **second step** is to examine whether the use of hedging in pro-GMO articles follows our inferred "scientific" occurrence patterns to a greater extent than the hedging in anti-GMO articles.

However, as our hedge classifier trained on the CoNLL dataset did not perform reliably on the different domain of prof-science vs. pop-science discussions of GMOs, we focus the main content of this paper on the first step. We describe data collection for the second step in the appendix.

3 Data

To accomplish the first step of our proposed procedure outlined above, we first constructed a prof-science/pop-science corpus by pulling text from Web of Science for prof-science examples and from LexisNexis for pop-science examples, as described in Section 3.1. Our corpus will be posted online at https://confluence.cornell.edu/display/llresearch/HedgingFramingGMOs.

As noted above, computing the degree of hedging in the aforementioned corpus requires access to a hedge-detection algorithm. We took a supervised approach, taking advantage of the availability of the CoNLL 2010 hedge-detection training and evaluation corpora, described in Section 3.2

3.1 Prof-science/pop-science data: LEXIS and WOS

As mentioned previously, a corpus of prof-science and pop-science articles is required to ascertain whether hedges are more prevalent in one or the

Dataset	Doc type	# docs	# sentences	Avg sentence length	Flesch reading ease
Prof-science/pop-science corpus					
WOS	abstracts	648	5596	22.35	23.39
LEXIS	(short) articles	928	36795	24.92	45.78
Hedge-detection corpora					
Bio (train)	abstracts, articles	1273, 9	14541 (18% uncertain)	29.97	20.77
Bio (eval)	articles	15	5003 (16% uncertain)	31.30	30.49
Wiki (train)	paragraphs	2186	11111 (22% uncertain)	23.07	35.23
Wiki (eval)	paragraphs	2346	9634 (23% uncertain)	20.82	31.71

Table 1: Basic descriptive statistics for the main corpora we worked with. We created the first two. Higher Flesch scores indicate text that is easier to read.

other of these two writing styles. Since our ultimate goal is to look at discourse related to GMOs, we restrict our attention to documents on this topic.

Thomson Reuter's Web of Science (WOS), a database of scientific journal and conference articles, was used as a source of prof-science samples. We chose to collect abstracts, rather than full scientific articles, because intuition suggests that the language in abstracts is more high-level than that in the bodies of papers, and thus more similar to the language one would see in a public debate on GMOs. To select for on-topic abstracts, we used the phrase "transgenic foods" as a search keyword and discarded results containing any of a hand-selected list of off-topic filtering terms (e.g., "mice" or "rats"). We then made use of domain expertise to manually remove off-topic texts. The process yielded 648 documents for a total of 5596 sentences.

Our source of pop-science articles was Lexis-Nexis (LEXIS). On-topic documents were collected from US newspapers using the search keywords "genetically modified foods" or "transgenic crops" and then imposing the additional requirement that at least two terms on a hand-selected list[7] be present in each document. After the removal of duplicates and texts containing more than 2000 words to delete excessively long articles, our final pop-science subcorpus was composed of 928 documents.

3.2 CoNLL hedge-detection training data [8]

As described in Farkas et al. (2010), the motivation behind the CoNLL 2010 shared task is that "distinguishing factual and uncertain information in texts is of essential importance in information extraction". As "uncertainty detection is extremely important for biomedical information extraction", one component of the dataset is biological abstracts and full articles from the BioScope corpus (Bio). Meanwhile, the chief editors of Wikipedia have drawn the attention of the public to specific markers of uncertainty known as weasel words[9]: they are words or phrases "aimed at creating an impression that something specific and meaningful has been said", when, in fact, "only a vague or ambiguous claim, or even a refutation, has been communicated". An example is "It has been claimed that ...": the claimant has not been identified, so the source of the claim cannot be verified. Thus, another part of the dataset is a set of Wikipedia articles (Wiki) annotated with weasel-word information. We view the combined Bio+Wiki corpus (henceforth the CoNLL dataset) as valuable for developing hedge detectors, and we attempt to study whether classifiers trained on this data can be generalized to other datasets.

3.3 Comparison

Table 1 gives the basic statistics on the main datasets we worked with. Though WOS and LEXIS differ in the total number of sentences, the average sentence length is similar. The average sentence length in Bio is longer than that in Wiki. The articles in WOS are markedly more difficult to read than the articles

[7]The term list: GMO, GM, GE, genetically modified, genetic modification, modified, modification, genetic engineering, engineered, bioengineered, franken, transgenic, spliced, G.M.O., tweaked, manipulated, engineering, pharming, aquaculture.

[8]http://www.inf.u-szeged.hu/rgai/conll2010st/

[9]http://en.wikipedia.org/wiki/Weasel_word

in LEXIS according to Flesch reading ease (Kincaid et al., 1975).

4 Hedging to distinguish scientific text: Initial annotation

As noted in Section 1, it is not a priori clear whether hedging distinguishes scientific text or that more hedges correspond to a more "scientific" discourse. To get an initial feeling for how frequently hedges occur in WOS and LEXIS, we hand-annotated a sample of sentences from each. In Section 4.1, we explain the annotation policy of the CoNLL 2010 Shared Task and our own annotation method for WOS and LEXIS. After that, we move forward in Section 4.2 to compare the percentage of uncertain sentences in prof-science vs. pop-science text on this small hand-labeled sample, and gain some evidence that there is indeed a difference in hedge occurrence rates, although, perhaps surprisingly, there seem to be more hedges in the *pop-science* texts.

As a side benefit, we subsequently use the hand-labeled sample we produce to investigate the accuracy of an automatic hedge detector in the WOS+LEXIS domain; more on this in Section 5.

4.1 Uncertainty annotation

CoNLL 2010 Shared Task annotation policy As described in Farkas et al. (2010, pg. 4), the data annotation polices for the CoNLL 2010 Shared Task were that "sentences containing at least one cue were considered as uncertain, while sentences with no cues were considered as factual", where a cue is a linguistic marker that *in context* indicates uncertainty. A straightforward example of a sentence marked "uncertain" in the Shared Task is 'Mild bladder wall thickening *raises the question of* cystitis.' The annotated cues are not necessarily general, particularly in Wiki, where some of the marked cues are as specific as '*some of schumann's best choral writing*', '*people of the jewish tradition*', or '*certain leisure or cultural activities*'.

Note that "uncertainty" in the Shared Task definition also encompassed phrasing that "creates an impression that something important has been said, but what is really communicated is vague, misleading, evasive or ambiguous ... [offering] an opinion without any backup or source". An example of such a sentence, drawn from Wikipedia and marked "uncertain" in the Shared Task, is 'Some people claim that this results in a better taste than that of other diet colas (most of which are sweetened with aspartame alone).'; Farkas et al. (2010) write, "The ... sentence does not specify the source of the information, it is just the vague term 'some people' that refers to the holder of this opinion".

Dataset	% of uncertain sentences
WOS	(estimated from 75-sentence sample) 20
LEXIS	(estimated from 78-sentence sample) 28
Bio	17
Wiki	23

Table 2: Percentages of uncertain sentences.

Our annotation policy We hand-annotated 200 randomly-sampled sentences, half from WOS and half from LEXIS[10], to gauge the frequency with which hedges occur in each corpus. Two annotators each followed the rules of the CoNLL 2010 Shared Task to label sentences as certain, uncertain, or not a proper sentence.[11] The annotators agreed on 153 proper sentences of the 200 sentences (75 from WOS and 78 from LEXIS). Cohen's Kappa (Fleiss, 1981) was 0.67 on the annotation, which means that the consistency between the two annotators was fair or good. However, there were some interesting cases where the two annotators could not agree. For example, in the sentence 'Cassava is the staple food of tropical Africa and its production, averaged over 24 countries, has increased more than threefold from 1980 to 2005 ... ', one of the annotators believed that "more than" made the sentence uncertain. These borderline cases indicate that the definition of hedging should be carefully delineated in future studies.

4.2 Percentages of uncertain sentences

To validate the hypothesis that prof-science articles contain more hedges, we computed the percentage

[10] We took steps to attempt to hide from the annotators any explicit clues as to the source of individual sentences: the subset of authors who did the annotation were not those that collected the data, and the annotators were presented the sentences in random order.

[11] The last label was added because of a few errors in scraping the data.

of uncertain sentences in our labeled data. As shown in Table 2, we observed a trend contradicting earlier studies. Uncertain sentences were more frequent in LEXIS than in WOS, though the difference was not statistically significant[12] (perhaps not surprising given the small sample size). The same trend was seen in the CoNLL dataset: there, too, the percentage of uncertain sentences was significantly smaller in Bio (prof-science articles) than in Wiki. In order to make a stronger argument about prof-science vs pop-science, however, more annotation on the WOS and LEXIS datasets is needed.

5 Experiments

As stated in Section 1, our proposal requires developing an effective hedge detection algorithm. Our approach for the preliminary work described in this paper is to re-implement Georgescul's (2010) algorithm; the experimental results on the Bio+Wiki domain, given in Section 5.1, are encouraging. Then we use this method to attempt to validate (at a larger scale than in our manual pilot annotation) whether hedges can be used to distinguish between prof-science and pop-science discourse on GMOs. Unfortunately, our results, given in Section 5.2, are inconclusive, since our trained model could not achieve satisfactory automatic hedge-detection accuracy on the WOS+LEXIS domain.

5.1 Method

We adopted the method of Georgescul (2010): Support Vector Machine classification based on a Gaussian Radial Basis kernel function (Vapnik, 1998; Fan et al., 2005), employing n-grams from annotated cue phrases as features, as described in more detail below. This method achieved the top performance in the CoNLL 2010 Wikipedia hedge-detection task (Farkas et al., 2010), and SVMs have been proven effective for many different applications. We used the LIBSVM toolkit in our experiments[13].

As described in Section 3.2, there are two separate datasets in the CoNLL dataset. We experimented on them separately (Bio, Wiki). Also, to make our classifier more generalizable to different datasets, we also trained models based on the two datasets combined (Bio+Wiki). As for features, we took advantage of the observation in Georgescul (2010) that the bag-of-words model does not work well for this task. We used different sets of features based on hedge *cue words* that have been annotated as part of the CoNLL dataset distribution[14]. The basic feature set was the frequency of each hedge cue word from the training corpus after removing stop words and punctuation and transforming words to lowercase. Then, we extracted unigrams, bigrams and trigrams from each hedge cue phrase. Table 3 shows the number of features in different settings. Notice that there are many more features in Wiki. As mentioned above, in Wiki, some cues are as specific as 'some of schumann's best choral writing', 'people of the jewish tradition', or ' certain leisure or cultural activities'. Taking n-grams from such specific cues can cause some sentences to be classified incorrectly.

Feature source	#features
Bio	220
Bio (cues + bigram + trigram)	340
Wiki	3740
Wiki (cues + bigram + trigram)	10603

Table 3: Number of features.

Best cross-validation performance				
Dataset	(C, γ)	P	R	F
Bio	$(40, 2^{-3})$	**84.0**	**92.0**	**87.8**
Wiki	$(30, 2^{-6})$	64.0	76.3	69.6
Bio+Wiki	$(10, 2^{-4})$	*66.7*	*78.3*	*72.0*

Table 4: Best 5-fold cross-validation performance for Bio and/or Wiki after parameter tuning. As a reminder, we repeat that our intended final test set is the WOS+LEXIS corpus, which is disjoint from Bio+Wiki.

We adopted several techniques from Georgescul (2010) to optimize performance through cross validation. Specifically, we tried different combinations of feature sets (the cue phrases themselves, cues +

[12] Throughout, "statistical significance" refers to the student t-test with $p < .05$.

[13] http://www.csie.ntu.edu.tw/~cjlin/libsvm/

[14] For the Bio model, we used cues extracted from Bio. Likewise, the Wiki model used cues from Wiki, and the Bio+Wiki model used cues from Bio+Wiki.

Evaluation set	Model	P	R	F
WOS+LEXIS	Bio	**54**	68	**60**
WOS+LEXIS	Wiki	38	54	45
WOS+LEXIS	Bio+Wiki	21	**93**	34
Sub-corpus performance of the model based on Bio				
WOS	Bio	58	73	65
LEXIS	Bio	52	64	57

Table 5: The upper part shows the performance on WOS and LEXIS based on models trained on the CoNLL dataset. The lower part gives the sub-corpus results for Bio, which provided the best performance on the full WOS+LEXIS corpus.

unigram, cues + bigram, cues + trigram, cues + unigram + bigram + trigram, cues + bigram + trigram). We tuned the width of the RBF kernel (γ) and the regularization parameter (C) via grid search over the following range of values: $\{2^{-9}, 2^{-8}, 2^{-7}, \ldots, 2^4\}$ for γ, $\{1, 10, 20, 30, \ldots, 150\}$ for C. We also tried different weighting strategies for negative and positive classes (i.e., either proportional to the number of positive instances, or uniform). We performed 5-fold cross validation for each possible combination of experimental settings on the three datasets (Bio, Wiki, Bio+Wiki).

Table 4 shows the best performance on all three datasets and the corresponding parameters. In the three datasets, cue+bigram+trigram provided the best performance, and the weighted model consistently produced superior results to the uniform model. The F1 measure for Bio was 87.8, which was satisfactory, while the F1 results for Wiki were 69.6, which were the worst of all the datasets. This resonates with our observation that the task on Wikipedia is more subtly defined and thus requires a more sophisticated approach than counting the occurrences of bigrams and trigrams.

5.2 Results on WOS+LEXIS

Next, we evaluated whether our best classifier trained on the CoNLL dataset can be generalized to other datasets, in particular, the WOS and LEXIS corpus. Performance was measured on the 153 sentences on which our annotators agreed, a dataset that was introduced in Section 4.1. Table 5 shows how the best models trained on Bio, Wiki, and Bio+Wiki, respectively, performed on the 153 labeled sentences. First, we can see that the performance degraded significantly compared to the performance for in-domain cross validation. Second, of the three different models, Bio showed the best performance. Bio+Wiki gave the worst performance, which hints that combining two datasets and cue words may not be a promising strategy: although Bio+Wiki shows very good recall, this can be attributed to its larger feature set, which contains all available cues and perhaps as a result has a very high false-positive rate. We further investigated and compared performance on LEXIS and WOS for the best model (Bio). Not surprisingly, our classifier works better in WOS than in LEXIS.

Evaluation set	(C, γ)	P	R	F
WOS + LEXIS	$(50, 2^{-9})$	68	62	65
WOS	$(50, 2^{-9})$	85	73	79
LEXIS	$(50, 2^{-9})$	57	54	56

Table 6: Best performance after parameter tuning based on the 153 labeled WOS+LEXIS sentences; this gives some idea of the upper-bound potential of our Georgescul-based method. The training set is Bio, which gave the best performance in Table 5.

It is clear that there exist domain differences between the CoNLL dataset and WOS+LEXIS. To better understand the poor cross-domain performance of the classifier, we tuned another model based on the performance on the 153 labeled sentences using Bio as training data. As we can see in Table 6, the performance on WOS improved significantly, while the performance on LEXIS decreased. This is probably caused by the fact that WOS is a collection of scientific paper abstracts, which is more similar to the training corpus than LEXIS, which is a collection of news media articles[15]. Also, LEXIS articles are hard to classify even with the tuned model, which challenges the effectiveness of a cue-words frequency approach beyond professional scientific texts. Indeed, the simplicity of our reimplementation of Georgescul's algorithm seems to cause longer sentences to be classified as uncertain, because cue phrases (or n-grams extracted from

[15]The Wiki model performed better on LEXIS than on WOS. Though the performance was not good, this result further reinforces the possibility of a domain-dependence problem.

cue phrases) are more likely to appear in lengthier sentences. Analysis of the best performing model shows that the false-positive sentences are significantly longer than the false-negative ones.[16]

Dataset	Model	% classified uncertain
WOS	Bio	16
LEXIS	Bio	19
WOS	Tuned	15
LEXIS	Tuned	14

Table 7: For completeness, we report here the percentage of uncertain sentences in WOS and LEXIS according to our trained classifiers, although we regard these results as unreliable since those classifiers have low accuracy. Bio refers to the best model trained on Bio only in Section 5.1, while Tuned refers to the model in Table 6 that is tuned based on the 153 labeled sentences in WOS+LEXIS.

While the cross-domain results were not reliable, we produced preliminary results on whether there exist fewer hedges in scientific text. We can see that the relative difference in certain/uncertain ratios predicted by the two different models (Bio, Tuned) are different in Table 7. In the tuned model, the difference between LEXIS and WOS in terms of the percentage of uncertain sentences was not statistically significant, while in the Bio model, their difference was statistically significant. Since the performance of our hedge classifier on the 153 hand-annotated WOS+LEXIS sentences was not reliable, though, we must abstain from making conclusive statements here.

6 Conclusion and future work

In this position paper, we advocated that researchers apply hedge detection not only to the classic motivation of information-extraction problems, but also to questions of how public opinion forms. We proposed a particular problem in how participants in debates frame their arguments. Specifically, we asked whether pro-GMO and anti-GMO articles differ in adopting a more "scientific" discourse. Inspired by earlier studies in social sciences relating hedging to texts aimed at professional scientists, we proposed addressing the question with automatic hedge detection as a first step. To develop a hedge classifier, we took advantage of the CoNLL dataset and a small annotated WOS and LEXIS dataset. Our preliminary results show there may exist a gap which indicates that hedging may, in fact, distinguish prof-science and pop-science documents. In fact, this computational analysis suggests the possibility that hedges occur less frequently in scientific prose, which contradicts several prior assertions in the literature.

To confirm the argument that pop-science tends to use more hedging than prof-science, we need a hedge classifier that performs more reliably in the WOS and LEXIS dataset than ours does. An interesting research direction would be to develop transfer-learning techniques to generalize hedge classifiers for different datasets, or to develop a general hedge classifier relatively robust to domain differences. In either case, more annotated data on WOS and LEXIS is needed for better evaluation or training.

Another strategy would be to bypass the first step, in which we determine whether hedges are more or less prominent in scientific discourse, and proceed directly to labeling and hedge-detection in pro-GMO and anti-GMO texts. However, this will not answer the question of whether advocates in debates other than on GMO-related topics employ a more scientific discourse. Nonetheless, to aid those who wish to pursue this alternate strategy, we have collected two sets of opinionated articles on GMO (pro- and anti-); see appendix for more details.

Acknowledgments We thank Daniel Hopkins and Bonnie Webber for reference suggestions, and the anonymous reviewers for helpful and thoughtful comments. This paper is based upon work supported in part by US NSF grants IIS-0910664 and IIS-1016099, a US NSF graduate fellowship to JS, Google, and Yahoo!

[16]Average length of true positive sentences : 28.6, false positive sentences 35.09, false negative sentences: 22.0.

References

Amr Ahmed and Eric P Xing. Staying informed: supervised and semi-supervised multi-view topical analysis of ideological perspective. In *EMNLP*, pages 1140–1150, 2010.

Charles Bazerman. *Shaping Written Knowledge:*

The Genre and Activity of the Experimental Article in Science. University of Wisconsin Press, Madison, Wis., 1988.

Beata Beigman Klebanov, Eyal Beigman, and Daniel Diermeier. Vocabulary choice as an indicator of perspective. In *ACL Short Papers*, pages 253–257, Stroudsburg, PA, USA, 2010. Association for Computational Linguistics.

Robert D. Benford and David A. Snow. Framing processes and social movements: An overview and assessment. *Annual Review of Sociology*, 26: 611–639, 2000.

Richard Harvey Brown. *Toward a democratic science: Scientific narration and civic communication*. Yale University Press, New Haven, 1998.

Dennis Chong and James N. Druckman. Framing theory. *Annual Review of Political Science*, 10: 103–126, 2007.

Jeanne Fahnestock. Accommodating Science. *Written Communication*, 3(3):275–296, 1986.

Jeanne Fahnestock. Preserving the figure: Consistency in the presentation of scientific arguments. *Written Communication*, 21(1):6–31, 2004.

Rong-En Fan, Pai-Hsuen Chen, and Chih-Jen Lin. Working set selection using second order information for training support vector machines. *JMLR*, 6:1889–1918, December 2005. ISSN 1532-4435.

Richárd Farkas, Veronika Vincze, György Móra, János Csirik, and György Szarvas. The CoNLL-2010 shared task: Learning to detect hedges and their scope in natural language text. In *CoNLL—Shared Task*, pages 1–12, 2010.

Joseph L. Fleiss. *Statistical Methods for Rates and Proportions*. Wiley series in probability and mathematical statistics. John Wiley & Sons, New York, second edition, 1981.

Maria Georgescul. A hedgehop over a max-margin framework using hedge cues. In *CONLL—Shared-Task*, pages 26–31, 2010.

G. Nigel Gilbert and Michael Joseph Mulkay. *Opening Pandora's box: A sociological analysis of scientists' discourse*. CUP Archive, 1984.

Erving Goffman. *Frame analysis: An essay on the organization of experience*. Harvard University Press, 1974.

Alan G. Gross. *The rhetoric of science*. Harvard University Press, Cambridge, Mass., 1990.

Michael Alexander Kirkwood Halliday and James R. Martin. *Writing science: Literacy and discursive power*. Psychology Press, London [u.a.], 1993.

Eric A Hardisty, Jordan Boyd-Graber, and Philip Resnik. Modeling perspective using adaptor grammars. In *EMNLP*, pages 284–292, 2010.

Ken Hyland. *Hedging in scientific research articles*. John Benjamins Pub. Co., Amsterdam; Philadelphia, 1998.

Napoleon K. Juanillo, Jr. Frames for Public Discourse on Biotechnology. In *Genetically Modified Food and the Consumer: Proceedings of the 13th meeting of the National Agricultural Biotechnology Council*, pages 39–50, 2001.

J. Peter Kincaid, Robert P. Fishburne, Richard L. Rogers, and Brad S. Chissom. Derivation of new readability formulas for navy enlisted personnel. Technical report, National Technical Information Service, Springfield, Virginia, February 1975.

George Lakoff. Hedges: A study in meaning criteria and the logic of fuzzy concepts. *Journal of Philosophical Logic*, 2(4):458–508, 1973.

Bruno Latour. *Science in action: How to follow scientists and engineers through society*. Harvard University Press, Cambridge, Mass., 1987.

Bruno Latour and Steve Woolgar. *Laboratory life: The social construction of scientific facts*. Sage Publications, Beverly Hills, 1979.

Beverly A. Lewin. Hedging: Form and function in scientific research texts. In *Genre Studies in English for Academic Purposes*, volume 9, pages 89–108. Universitat Jaume I, 1998.

Wei-Hao Lin, Theresa Wilson, Janyce Wiebe, and Alexander Hauptmann. Which side are you on? identifying perspectives at the document and sentence levels. In *CoNLL*, 2006.

Greg Myers. The pragmatics of politeness in scientific articles. *Applied Linguistics*, 10(1):1–35, 1989.

Greg Myers. Discourse studies of scientific popularization: Questioning the boundaries. *Discourse Studies*, 5(2):265–279, 2003.

Françoise Salager-Meyer. Scientific discourse and contrastive linguistics: hedging. *European Science Editing*, 37(2):35–37, 2011.

Dietram A. Scheufele. Framing as a theory of media effects. *Journal of Communication*, 49(1):103–122, 1999.

Vladimir N. Vapnik. *Statistical Learning Theory*. Wiley-Interscience, 1998.

Teppo Varttala. Remarks on the communicative functions of hedging in popular scientific and specialist research articles on medicine. *English for Specific Purposes*, 18(2):177–200, 1999.

Teppo Varttala. *Hedging in scientifically oriented discourse: Exploring variation according to discipline and intended audience*. PhD thesis, University of Tampere, 2001.

7 Appendix: pro- vs. anti-GMO dataset

Here, we describe the pro- vs. anti-GMO dataset we collected, in the hopes that this dataset may prove helpful in future research regarding the GMO debates, even though we did not use the corpus in the project described in this paper.

The second step of our overall procedure outlined in the introduction — that step being to examine whether the use of hedging in pro-GMO articles corresponds with our inferred "scientific" occurrence patterns more than that in anti-GMO articles — requires a collection of opinionated articles on GMOs. Our first attempt to use news media articles (LEXIS) was unsatisfying, as we found many articles attempt to maintain a neutral position. This led us to collect documents from more strongly opinionated organizational websites such as Greenpeace (anti-GMO), Non GMO Project (anti-GMO), or Why Biotechnology (pro-GMO). Articles were collected from 20 pro-GMO and 20 anti-GMO organizational web sites.

After the initial collection of data, near-duplicates and irrelevant articles were filtered through clustering, keyword searches and distance between word vectors at the document level. We have collected 762 "anti" documents and 671 "pro" documents. We reduced this to a 404 "pro" and 404 "con" set as follows. Each retained "document" consists of only the first 200 words after excluding the first 50 words of documents containing over 280 words. This was done to avoid irrelevant sections such as *Educators have permission to reprint articles for classroom use; other users, please contact editor@actionbioscience.org for reprint permission. See reprint policy.*

The data will be posted online at https://confluence.cornell.edu/display/llresearch/HedgingFramingGMOs.

Recognizing Arguing Subjectivity and Argument Tags

Alexander Conrad, Janyce Wiebe, and Rebecca Hwa
Department of Computer Science
University of Pittsburgh
Pittsburgh PA, 15260, USA
{conrada,wiebe,hwa}@cs.pitt.edu

Abstract

In this paper we investigate two distinct tasks. The first task involves detecting arguing subjectivity, a type of linguistic subjectivity on which relatively little work has yet to be done. The second task involves labeling instances of arguing subjectivity with argument tags reflecting the conceptual argument being made. We refer to these two tasks collectively as "recognizing arguments". We develop a new annotation scheme and assemble a new annotated corpus to support our learning efforts. Through our machine learning experiments, we investigate the utility of a sentiment lexicon, discourse parser, and semantic similarity measures with respect to recognizing arguments. By incorporating information gained from these resources, we outperform a unigram baseline by a significant margin. In addition, we explore a two-phase approach to recognizing arguments, with promising results.

1 Introduction

Subjectivity analysis is a thriving field within natural language processing. However, most research into subjectivity has focused on sentiment with respect to concrete things such as product debates (e.g., (Somasundaran and Wiebe, 2009), (Yu et al., 2011)) and movie reviews (e.g., (He et al., 2011), (Maas et al., 2011), (Pang and Lee, 2004)). Analysis often follows the opinion-target paradigm, in which expressions of sentiment are assessed with respect to the aspects of the object(s) under consideration towards which they are targeted. For example, in the domain of smartphone reviews, aspects could include product features such as the keyboard, screen quality, and battery life.

Although sentiment analysis is interesting and important in its own right, this paradigm does not seem to be the best match for fine-grained analysis of ideological domains. While sentiment is also present in documents from this domain, previous work (Somasundaran and Wiebe, 2010) has found that arguing subjectivity, a less-studied form of subjectivity, is more frequently employed and more relevant for a robust assessment of ideological positions. Whereas sentiment conveys the polarity of a writer's affect towards a topic, arguing subjectivity is a type of linguistic subjectivity in which a person expresses a controversial belief about what is true or what action ought to be taken regarding a central contentious issue (Somasundaran, 2010). For example, consider this sentence about health care reform:

> (1) Almost everyone knows that we must start holding insurance companies accountable and give Americans a greater sense of stability and security when it comes to their health care.

In a traditional opinion-target or sentiment-topic paradigm, perhaps this sentence could be labeled as containing a negative sentiment towards a topic representing "insurance companies", or a positive sentiment towards a topic representing "stability" or "security". However, a reader of a political editorial or blog may be more interested in *why* the author is negative towards insurers, and *how* the author proposes to improve stability of the healthcare system. By focusing on the arguments conveyed through arguing subjectivity, we aim to capture these kind of conceptual reasons an author provides when arguing for his or her position.

However, identifying when someone is arguing is only part of the challenge. Since arguing subjectivity is used to express arguments, the next natural step is to identify the argument being expressed through each instance of arguing subjectivity. To illustrate this distinction, consider the following three example spans:

> (2) the bill is a job destroyer
> (3) President Obamas signature domestic policy will throw 100,000 people out of work come January
> (4) he can't expand his business because he can't afford the burden of Obamacare

Each of these examples contains arguing subjectivity, but more importantly, each expresses roughly the same idea, namely, that the recently-passed health care reform bill will cause economic harm. This latent, shared idea giving rise to each of the three spans is what we mean by "argument tag".

However, although all three are related, example spans (2) and (3) are more similar than (4) in terms of the notions they convey: while the first two explicitly are concerned with the loss of jobs, the last focuses on business expansion and the economy as a whole. If we were to tag these three spans with respect to the argument that each is making, should they all receive the same tag, or should (4)'s tag be different?

To address these challenges, we propose in this work a new annotation scheme for identifying arguing subjectivity and a hierarchical model for organizing "argument tags". In our hierarchical model, (4) would receive a different tag from (2) and (3), but because of the tags' relatedness all would share the same parent tag.

In addition to presenting this new scheme for labeling arguing subjectivity, we also explore sentiment, discourse, and distributional similarity as tools to enhance identification and classification of arguing subjectivity. Finally, we also investigate splitting the arguing subjectivity detection task up into two distinct phases: identifying expressions of arguing subjectivity, and labelling each such expression with an appropriate argument tag.

Since no corpora annotated for arguing subjectivity yet exist, we gather and annotate a corpus of blog posts and op-eds about a controversial topic, namely, the recently-passed "ObamaCare" health care reform bill.

2 Annotation Scheme

We designed our annotation scheme with two goals in mind: identifying all spans of text which express arguing subjectivity, and labelling each such span with an argument tag. To address the first goal, our annotators manually identified and annotated spans of text containing arguing subjectivity using the GATE environment[1]. Annotators were instructed to identify spans of 1 sentence or less in which a writer "conveys a controversial private state concerning what she believes to be true or what action she believes should be taken" concerning the health care reform debate. To train our annotators to recognize arguing subjectivity, we performed several rounds of practice on a separate dataset. Between each round, our annotators met to discuss their annotations and resolve disagreements.

As a heuristic to help distinguish between borderline sentences, we advised our annotators to imagine disputants from each side writing the sentence in isolation. If a disputant from either side could conceivably write the sentence, then the sentence is likely objective. For example, statements of accepted facts and statistics generally fall into this category. However, if only one side could conceivably be the author of the sentence, it is highly likely that the sentence expresses a controversial belief relevant to the debate and thus should be labeled as subjective.

Next, the annotators labeled each arguing span with an argument tag. As illustrated in earlier examples, an argument tag represents a

[1] `http://gate.ac.uk/`

controversial abstract belief expressed through arguing subjectivity. Since the meanings of many tags may be related, we organize these tags in a hierarchical "stance structure". A stance structure is a tree-based data structure containing all of the argument tags associated with a particular debate, organizing those tags using "is-a" relationships. Our stance structure contains two levels of argument tags: upper-level "primary" argument tags and lower-level "secondary" tags. Each primary tag has one of the stances (either "pro" or "anti" in our case) as its parent, while each secondary tag has a primary tag as its parent[2].

Political science "arguing dimension" approaches to debate framing analysis served, in part, as an inspiration for our stance structure (Baumgartner et al., 2008). Also, as illustrated in Section 1, this approach permits us additional flexibility, supporting classification at different levels of specificity depending on the task at hand and the amount of data available. We envision a future scenario in which a community of users collaboratively builds a stance structure to represent a new topic or debate, or in which analysts build a stance structure to categorize the issues expressed towards a proposed law, such as in the context of e-rulemaking (Cardie et al., 2008).

Because each stance contains a large number of argument tags, we back-off from each secondary argument tag to its primary argument parent for the classification experiments. We chose to do this in order to ensure that we have a sufficient amount of data with which to train the classifier.

3 Dataset

For this study, we chose to focus on online editorials and blog posts concerning the ongoing debate over health insurance reform legislation in the United States. Our intuition is that blogs and editorials represent a genre rich in both subjectivity and arguments. We collected documents written both before and after the passage of the final "Patient Protection and Affordable Care Act" bill using the "Google Blog Search"[3] and "Daily Op Ed"[4] search portals. By choosing a relatively broad time window, from early 2009 to late 2011, we aimed to capture a wide range of arguments expressed throughout the debate.

The focus of this paper is on sentence-level argument detection rather than document-level stance classification (e.g., (Anand et al., 2011), (Park et al., 2011), (Somasundaran and Wiebe, 2010), (Burfoot et al., 2011)). We treat stance classification as a separate step preceding arguing subjectivity detection, and thus provide oracle stance labels for our data.

We treat documents written from the "pro"

"pro" documents	37
"pro" sentences	1,222
"anti" documents	47
"anti" sentences	1,456
total documents	84
total sentences	2,678

Table 1: Dataset summary statistics.

arguing subjectivity	
objective	683
subjective	588

argument labels	
no label	683
improves_healthcare_access	130
improves_healthcare_affordability	104
people_dont_know_truth_about_bill	75
controls_healthcare_costs	54
improves_quality_of_healthcare	52
helps_economy	51
bill_should_be_passed	43
other argument	79

Table 2: Arguing and argument label statistics for the "pro" stance.

[2]Our stance structure contains an additional "aspect" level consisting of a-priori categories adopted from political science research. However, we do not utilize this level of the stance structure in this work.

[3]`http://www.google.com/blogsearch`

[4]`http://www.dailyoped.com/`

arguing subjectivity	
objective	913
subjective	575

argument labels	
no label	913
diminishes_quality_of_care	122
too_expensive	67
unpopular	60
hurts_economy	55
expands_govt	52
bill_is_politically_motivated	44
other_reforms_more_appropriate	35
other argument	140

Table 3: Arguing and argument label statistics for the "anti" stance.

stance and documents written from the "anti" stance as separate datasets. Being written from different positions, the two stances will have different argument labels and may employ different styles of arguing subjectivity. Table 1 provides an overview of the size of this dataset. Summary statistics concerning the density of arguing and argument labels in the two sides of the dataset is presented in Tables 2 and 3. However, since it can be difficult to summarize a complex argument in a short phrase, many of these labels by themselves do not clearly convey the meaning they are meant to represent. To better illustrate the meanings of some of the more ambiguous labels, Table 4 presents several annotated example spans for some of the more unclear ambiguous argument labels.

4 Agreement Study

One of our authors performed annotation of our corpus, the broad outlines of which are sketched in the previous section. However, to assess inter-annotator agreement for this annotation scheme, we recruited a non-author to independently annotate a subset of our corpus consisting of 384 sentences across 10 documents. This non-author both identified spans of arguing subjectivity and assigned argument tags. She was given a stance structure from which to select argument tags.

improves_healthcare_access
"Our reform will prohibit insurance companies from denying coverage because of your medical history."
"Let's also not overlook the news from last week about the millions of younger Americans who are getting coverage thanks to consumer protections that are now in place."
improves_healthcare_affordability
" new health insurance exchanges will offer competitive, consumer-centered health insurance marketplaces..."
"Millions of seniors can now afford medication they would otherwise struggle to pay for."
people_dont_know_truth_about_bill
"...the cynics and the naysayers will continue to exploit fear and concerns for political gain."
"Republican leaders, who see opportunities to gain seats in the elections, have made clear that they will continue to peddle fictions about a government takeover of the health care system and about costs too high to bear."
unpopular
"The 1,000-page monstrosity that emerged in various editions from Congress was done in by widespread national revulsion..."
"Support for ObamaCare's repeal is broad, and includes one group too often overlooked during the health care debate: America's doctors."
expands_govt
"...the real goal of the health care overhaul was to enact the largest entitlement program in history..."
"the new bureaucracy the health care legislation creates is so complex and indiscriminate that its size and cost is 'currently unknowable.' "
bill_is_politically_motivated
"...tawdry backroom politics were used to sell off favors in exchange for votes."
"From the wildly improper gifts to senators like Nebraska's Ben Nelson to this week's backroom deals for unions..."

Table 4: Example annotated spans for several argument labels.

metric	recall	precision	f-measure
agr	0.677	0.690	0.683

kappa for overlapping annotations	0.689

Table 5: Inter-annotator span *agr* (top) and argument label kappa on overlapping spans (bottom).

In assessing inter-annotator agreement on this subset of the corpus, we must address two levels of agreement, arguing spans and argument tags.

At first glance, how to assess agreement of annotated arguing spans is not obvious. Because our annotation scheme did not enforce strict boundaries, we hypothesized that both annotators would both frequently see an instance of arguing subjectivity within a local region of text, but would disagree with respect to where the arguing begins and ends. Thus, we adopt from (Wilson and Wiebe, 2003) the *agr* directional agreement metric to measure the degree of annotation overlap. Given two sets of spans A and B annotated by two different annotators, this metric measures the fraction of spans in A which at least partially overlap with any spans in B. Specifically, agreement is computed as:

$$agr(A \,||\, B) = \frac{|\, A \text{ matching } B \,|}{|\, A \,|}$$

When A is the gold standard set of annotations, *agr* is equivalent to recall. Similarly, when B is the gold standard, *agr* is equivalent to precision. For this evaluation, we treat the dataset annotated by our primary annotator as the gold standard. Table 5 presents these *agr* scores and f-measures for the arguing spans.

Second, we measure agreement with respect to the argument tags assigned by the two annotators. Continuing to follow the methodology of (Wilson and Wiebe, 2003), we look at each pair of annotations, one from each annotator, which share at least a partial overlap. For each such pair, we assess whether the two spans share the same primary argument tag. Scores for primary argument label agreement in terms of Cohen's kappa are also presented in Table 5. Since this kappa score falls within the range of $0.67 \leq K \leq 0.8$, according to Krippendorf's scale (Krippendorff, 2004) this allows us to draw tentative conclusions concerning a significant level of tag agreement.

5 Methods

As discussed earlier, recognizing arguments can be thought of in terms of two related but different tasks: recognizing a type of subjectivity, and labeling instances of that subjectivity with tags. We refer to the binary arguing subjectivity detection task as "arg", and to the multi-class argument labeling task as "tag". For the "tag" task, we create eight classes: one for each of the seven most-frequent labels, and an eighth into which we agglomerate the remaining less-frequent labels. We only consider the sentences known to be subjective (via oracle information) for the "tag" task.

We also perform a "combined" task. This third task is conceptually similar to the "tag" task, except that all sentences are considered rather than only the subjective sentences. In addition to the eight classes used by "tag", "combined" adds an additional class for non-arguing sentences. Finally, we also perform a two-stage "arg+tag" task. In this two-stage task, the instances labeled as subjective by the "arg" classifier are passed as input to the "tag" classifier. The intuition behind this two-phase approach is that the features most useful for identifying arguing subjectivity may not be the most useful for discriminating between argument tags, and vice versa. For all of our classification tasks, we treat both the "pro" and "anti" stances separately, building separate classifiers for each stance for each of the above tasks.

In general, we perform single-label classification at the sentence level. However, sentences containing multiple labels pose a challenge. Since this was an early exploratory work on a very difficult task, we decided to handle this situation by splitting sentences containing multiple labels into separate instances for the purpose of learning, assigning a single label to each instance. However, only about 3% of the sentences in our corpus contained multiple labels. Thus, replacing this splitting step in the future with another method that does not require oracle information, such as choosing the label which covers the most words in the sentence, is a reasonable simplification of the task.

Since discourse actions, such as contrasting, restating, and identifying causation, play a substantial role in arguing, we hypothesize that information about the discourse roles played by a span of text will help improve classification. Although discourse parsers historically haven't been found to be effective for subjectivity analysis, a new parser (Lin et al., 2010) trained on the Penn Discourse TreeBank (PDTB) tagset (Prasad et al., 2008) has recently been released. Previous work has demonstrated that this parser can reliably detect discourse relationships between adjacent sentences (Lin et al., 2011), and the PDTB tagset, being relatively flat, is conducive to feature engineering for our task.

To give a feeling for the kind of discourse relations identified by this parser, the following example illustrates a concession relation identified in the corpus by the parser. The italicized text represents the concession, while the bolded text indicates the overall point that the author is making. The underlined word was identified by the parser as an explicit concessionary clue.

> (7) the health care reform legislation that President Obama now seems likely to sign into law , while *an unlovely mess* , **will be remembered as a landmark accomplishment** .

Using this automatic information, we define features indicating the discourse relationships by which the instance is connected to surrounding text. Specifically, the class of discourse relationship connecting the target instance to the previous instance, the relationship connecting it to the following instance, and any internal discourse relationships by which the parts of the instance are connected to each other are each added as features. Since PDTB contains many fine-grained discourse relations, we replace each discourse relationship type inferred by the discourse parser with the parent top-level PDTB discourse relationship class. We arrive at a total of 15 binary discourse relationship features: (4 top-level classes + "other") x (connects to previous + connects to following + internal connection) = 15. We refer to these features as "rels".

As illustrated in our earlier examples, while arguing subjectivity is different from sentiment, the two types of subjectivity are often related. Thus, we investigate incorporating sentiment information based on the presence of unigram clues from a publically-available sentiment lexicon[5] (Wilson, 2005). Each clue in the lexicon is marked as being either "strong" or "weak".

We found that this lexicon was producing many false hits for positive sentiment. Thus, a span containing a minimum of two positive clues of which at least one is marked as "strong", or three positive "weak" clues, is augmented with a feature indicating positive sentiment. For negative sentiment the threshold is slightly lower, at one "strong" clue or two "weak" clues. These features are referred to as "senti".

A challenge to argument tag assignment is the broad diversity of language through which individual entities or specific actions may be referenced, as illustrated in Examples (2-4) from Section 1. To address this problem, we investigate expanding each instance with terms that are most similar, according to a distributional model generated from Wikipedia articles, to the nouns and verbs present within the instance (Pantel et al., 2009). We refer to these features as "exp$n$", where n is the number of most-similar terms with which to expand the instance for each noun or verb. We experiment with values of $n = 5$ and $n = 10$.

Subjectivity classification of small units of text, such as individual microblog posts (Jiang et al., 2011) and sentences (Riloff et al., 2003), has been shown to benefit from additional context. Thus, we augment the feature representation of each target sentence with features from the two preceding and two following sentences. These additional features are modified so that they do not fall within the same feature space

[5]downloaded from `http://www.cs.pitt.edu/mpqa/subj_lexicon.html`

feat. abbrev.	elaboration
unigram	
senti	2 binary features indicating positive or negative sentiment based on presence of lexicon clues
rels	15 binary features indicating kinds of discourse relationships and how they connect instance to surrounding text
exp5	for each noun and verb in instance, expand instance with top 5 most distributionally similar words
exp10	for each noun and verb in instance, expand instance with top 10 most distributionally similar words

Table 6: Overview of features used in the arguing and argument experiments.

features	arg	tag	comb.
unigram baseline	0.610	0.425	0.458
senti	0.614	0.426	0.459
rels	0.614	0.422	0.462
senti, rels	0.618	0.424	0.465
exp5	*0.635*	**0.522**	*0.482*
exp5, senti	**0.638**	**0.515**	**0.486**
exp5, rels	**0.640**	**0.522**	*0.484*
exp5, senti, rels	**0.643**	**0.516**	*0.484*
exp10	**0.645**	**0.517**	**0.488**
exp10, senti	**0.647**	**0.515**	**0.489**
exp10, rels	**0.642**	**0.512**	**0.490**
exp10, senti, rels	**0.644**	**0.513**	**0.490**

Table 7: Classifier accuracy for differing feature sets. Significant improvement ($p < 0.05$) over baseline is boldfaced ($0.05 < p < 0.1$ italicized). Underline indicates best performance per column.

as the features representing the target sentence.

Using the Naive Bayes classifier within the WEKA machine learning toolkit (Hall et al., 2009), we explore the impact of the features described above on our four experiment configurations. We perform our experiments using k-fold cross-validation, where k equals the number of documents within the stance. The test set for each fold consists of a single document's instances. For the "pro" dataset $k = 37$, while for the "anti" dataset $k = 47$.

6 Results

Table 7 presents the accuracy scores from each of our stand-alone classifiers across combinations of feature sets. Each feature set consists of unigrams augmented with the designated additional features, as described in Section 5. To evaluate the "tag" classifier in isolation, we use oracle information to provide this classifier with only the subjective instances. To assess significance of the performance differences between feature sets, we used the Pearson Chi-squared test with Yates continuity correction.

Expansion of nouns and verbs with distributionally-similar terms ("exp5", "exp10") plays the largest role in improving classifier performance. While differences between configurations using "exp5" versus "exp10" were generally not significant, all of the configurations incorporating some version of term expansion outperformed the unigram baseline by either a statistically significant margin ($p < 0.05$) or by a margin that approached significance ($0.05 < p < 0.1$).

Sentiment features consistently produce improvements in accuracy for the "arg" and "combined" tasks. While these improvements are promising, the lack of a significant margin of improvement when incorporating sentiment is surprising. Since sentiment lexicons are known to be highly domain-dependent (Pan et al., 2010), it may be the case that, having been learned from a general news corpus, the sentiment lexicon employed in this work is not the best match for the domain of "ObamaCare" blogs and editorials. Similarly, the discourse features also fail to produce significant improvements in accuracy.

Finally, we aim to test our hypothesis that separating the "arg" and "tag" phases results in improvement beyond treating the two in a single "combined" phase. The first step of our hierarchy involves normal classification of all sentences using the "arg" classifier. Next, all sentences judged to contain arguing subjectivity by "arg"

arg features	tag features	acc.
exp5, senti, rels	exp5	0.506
	exp5, rels	0.506
	exp10	0.501
exp10	exp5	*0.514*
	exp5, rels	0.513
	exp10	0.512
exp10, senti	exp5	*0.514*
	exp5, rels	0.513
	exp10	0.512

Table 8: Accuracies of two-stage classifiers across different combinations of feature sets for the "arg" and "tag" phases. Italics indicate improvement over the top "combined" configuration which approaches significance ($0.05 < p < 0.1$). Underline indicates best overall performance.

are passed to the "tag" classifier to have an argument tag assigned. We choose three promising feature sets for the "arg" and "tag" phases, based on best performance in isolation.

Results of this hierarchical experiment are presented in Table 8. We evaluate the hierarchical system against the best-performing "combined" single-phase systems from Table 7. While all of the hierarchical configurations beat the best "combined" classifier, none beats the top combined classifier by a significant margin, although the best configurations approach significance ($0.05 < p < 0.1$).

7 Related Work

Much recent work in ideological subjectivity detection has focused on detecting a writer's stance in domains of varying formality, such as online forums, debating websites, and op-eds. (Anand et al., 2011) demonstrates the usefulness of dependency relations, LIWC counts (Pennebaker et al., 2001), and information about related posts for this task. (Lin et al., 2006) explores relationships between sentence-level and document-level classification for a stance-like prediction task.

Among the literature on ideological subjectivity, perhaps most similar to our work is (Somasundaran and Wiebe, 2010). This paper investigates the impact of incorporating arguing-based and sentiment-based features into binary stance prediction for debate posts. Also closely related to our work is (Somasundaran et al., 2007). To support answering of opinion-based questions, this work investigates the use of high-precision sentiment and arguing clues for sentence-level sentiment and arguing prediction.

Another active area of related research focuses on identifying important aspects towards which sentiment is expressed within a domain. (He et al., 2011) approaches this problem through topic modeling, extending the joint sentiment-topic (JST) model which aims to simultaneously learn sentiment and aspect probabilities for a unit of text. (Yu et al., 2011) takes a different approach, investigating thesaurus methods for learning aspects based on groups of synonymous nouns within product reviews.

8 Conclusion

In this paper, we explored recognizing arguments in terms of arguing subjectivity and argument tags. We presented and evaluated a new annotation scheme to capture arguing subjectivity and argument tags, and annotated a new dataset. Utilizing existing sentiment, discourse, and distributional similarity resources, we explored ways in which these three forms of knowledge could be used to enhance argument recognition. In particular, our empirical results highlight the important role played by distributional similarity in all phases of detecting arguing subjectivity and argument tags. We have also provided tentative evidence suggesting that addressing the problem of recognizing arguments in two separate phases may be beneficial to overall classification accuracy.

9 Acknowledgments

This material is based in part upon work supported by National Science Foundation award #0916046. We would like to thank Patrick Pantel for sharing his thesaurus of distributionally similar words from Wikipedia with us, Amber Boydstun for insightful conversations about debate frame categorization, and the anonymous reviewers for their useful feedback.

References

Pranav Anand, Marilyn Walker, Rob Abbott, Jean E. Fox Tree, Robeson Bowmani, and Michael Minor. 2011. Cats rule and dogs drool!: Classifying stance in online debate. In *WASSA*, pages 1–9, Portland, Oregon, June.

F.R. Baumgartner, S.D. Boef, and A.E. Boydstun. 2008. *The decline of the death penalty and the discovery of innocence*. Cambridge University Press.

Clinton Burfoot, Steven Bird, and Timothy Baldwin. 2011. Collective classification of congressional floor-debate transcripts. In *ACL*, pages 1506–1515, Portland, Oregon, USA, June.

Claire Cardie, Cynthia Farina, Adil Aijaz, Matt Rawding, and Stephen Purpura. 2008. A study in rule-specific issue categorization for e-rulemaking. In *DG.O*, pages 244–253.

Mark Hall, Eibe Frank, Geoffrey Holmes, Bernhard Pfahringer, Peter Reutemann, and Ian H. Witten. 2009. The weka data mining software: an update. *SIGKDD Explor. Newsl.*, 11:10–18, November.

Yulan He, Chenghua Lin, and Harith Alani. 2011. Automatically extracting polarity-bearing topics for cross-domain sentiment classification. In *ACL*, pages 123–131, Portland, Oregon, USA, June.

Long Jiang, Mo Yu, Ming Zhou, Xiaohua Liu, and Tiejun Zhao. 2011. Target-dependent twitter sentiment classification. In *ACL*, pages 151–160, Portland, Oregon, USA, June.

K. Krippendorff. 2004. *Content analysis: an introduction to its methodology*. Sage.

Wei-Hao Lin, Theresa Wilson, Janyce Wiebe, and Alexander Hauptmann. 2006. Which side are you on?: identifying perspectives at the document and sentence levels. In *CoNLL*, pages 109–116.

Ziheng Lin, Hwee Tou Ng, and Min-Yen Kan. 2010. A pdtb-styled end-to-end discourse parser. *CoRR*.

Ziheng Lin, Hwee Tou Ng, and Min-Yen Kan. 2011. Automatically evaluating text coherence using discourse relations. In *ACL*, pages 997–1006, Portland, Oregon, USA, June.

Andrew L. Maas, Raymond E. Daly, Peter T. Pham, Dan Huang, Andrew Y. Ng, and Christopher Potts. 2011. Learning word vectors for sentiment analysis. In *ACL*, pages 142–150, Portland, Oregon, USA, June.

Sinno Jialin Pan, Xiaochuan Ni, Jian tao Sun, Qiang Yang, and Zheng Chen. 2010. Cross-domain sentiment classification via spectral feature alignment. In *WWW*.

Bo Pang and Lillian Lee. 2004. A sentimental education: Sentiment analysis using subjectivity summarization based on minimum cuts. In *ACL*, pages 271–278, Barcelona, Spain, July.

Patrick Pantel, Eric Crestan, Arkady Borkovsky, Ana-Maria Popescu, and Vishnu Vyas. 2009. Web-scale distributional similarity and entity set expansion. In *EMNLP*, pages 938–947, Morristown, NJ, USA.

Souneil Park, Kyung Soon Lee, and Junehwa Song. 2011. Contrasting opposing views of news articles on contentious issues. In *ACL*, pages 340–349, Portland, Oregon, USA, June.

James W Pennebaker, Roger J Booth, and Martha E Francis. 2001. Linguistic inquiry and word count (liwc): Liwc2001. *Linguistic Inquiry*, (Mahwah, NJ):0.

Rashmi Prasad, Nikhil Dinesh, Alan Lee, Eleni Miltsakaki, Livio Robaldo, Aravind Joshi, and Bonnie Webber. 2008. The penn discourse treebank 2.0. In *LREC*, May.

Ellen Riloff, Janyce Wiebe, and Theresa Wilson. 2003. Learning subjective nouns using extraction pattern bootstrapping. In *CoNLL*, pages 25–32.

Swapna Somasundaran and Janyce Wiebe. 2009. Recognizing stances in online debates. In *ACL-AFNLP*, pages 226–234.

Swapna Somasundaran and Janyce Wiebe. 2010. Recognizing stances in ideological on-line debates. In *CAAGET*, pages 116–124.

Swapna Somasundaran, Theresa Wilson, Janyce Wiebe, and Veselin Stoyanov. 2007. Qa with attitude: Exploiting opinion type analysis for improving question answering in on-line discussions and the news. In *ICWSM*.

Swampa Somasundaran. 2010. *Discourse-Level Relations for Opinion Analysis*. Ph.D. thesis, University of Pittsburgh, USA.

Theresa Wilson and Janyce Wiebe. 2003. Annotating opinions in the world press. In *SIGdial*, pages 13–22.

Theresa Wilson. 2005. Recognizing contextual polarity in phrase-level sentiment analysis. In *EMNLP*, pages 347–354.

Jianxing Yu, Zheng-Jun Zha, Meng Wang, and Tat-Seng Chua. 2011. Aspect ranking: Identifying important product aspects from online consumer reviews. In *ACL*, pages 1496–1505, Portland, Oregon, USA, June.

Author Index